Student Brains, School Issues:
A Collection of Articles

Edited by
Robert Sylwester
UNIVERSITY OF OREGON

PEARSON
SkyLight

Glenview, Illinois

Student Brains, School Issues: A Collection of Articles

Published by Pearson Professional Development
1900 E. Lake Ave., Glenview, IL 60025
Phone 800-348-4474, 847-657-7450
FAX 847-486-3183
info@pearsonpd.com
http://www.pearsonpd.com

ISBN 1-57517-046-9
LCCN: 98-060561

2108-V

Z Y X W V U T S R Q P O N M L K J I H G F
06 05 04 03   15 14 13 12 11 10 9 8

Contents

Introduction v

**SECTION 1: EDUCATION AND THE CURRENT COGNITIVE
SCIENCE REVOLUTION** 1

- On Using Knowledge About Our Brain: A Conversation with
  Bob Sylwester
  by Ron Brandt 3
- Smart Brains
  by Rebecca Jones 9
- Recommended Readings 18

**SECTION 2: THE EMERGENCE AND IMPORTANCE
OF EMOTION** 19

- On Emotional Intelligence: A Conversation with Daniel
  Goleman
  by John O'Neil 21
- How Emotions Affect Learning
  by Robert Sylwester 29
- The Neurobiology of Self-Esteem and Aggression
  by Robert Sylwester 41
- Can't Do Without Love
  by Shannon Brownlee 51
- Recommended Readings 56

**SECTION 3: BIOLOGICAL AND TECHNOLOGICAL
PERSPECTIVES ON INTELLIGENCE** 59

- The First Seven . . . and the Eighth: A Conversation with
  Howard Gardner
  by Kathy Checkley 61

- What Does It Mean to Be Smart?
  by Robert J. Sternberg 71
- Bioelectronic Learning: The Effects of Electronic Media on a Developing Brain
  by Robert Sylwester 81
- Forecasts for Technology in Education
  by David Moursund 89
- Recommended Readings 101

SECTION 4: NEW PERSPECTIVES ON COMPUTATIONAL THOUGHT PROCESSES 103
- A Brain That Talks
  by Jo Ann C. Gutin 105
- Why Andy Couldn't Read
  by Pat Wingert and Barbara Kantrowitz 119
- A Head for Numbers
  by Robert Kunzig 129
- New Research on the Brain: Implications for Instruction
  by Douglas Carnine 143
- Recommended Readings 159

Authors 161

Acknowledgments 163

Index 167

Introduction

Student Brains, School Issues: A Collection of Articles

Education is at the edge of a major transformation. Recent dramatic advances in the brain sciences and computer technology are moving us toward a new perspective of what it means to be and to teach a human being.

THE BRAIN SCIENCES

Brain imaging technology monitors can now display the activity of a normal human brain while it responds to problems posed by researchers. For example, as a subject reads, writes, or plays a computer game a monitor simultaneously shows the activity level of various brain areas associated with the activity. Scientists, thus, are determining how and where our brain processes a wide range of educationally significant cognitive tasks. These studies focus primarily on the identification, organization, and operation of the vast number of neural network systems that interconnect the 100 billion neurons in our brain and on the dozens of neurotransmitter and hormonal systems that regulate the activities of neural networks. Such studies will lead to a better understanding of changes that occur within our brains while we're learning something and of the differences among individuals or groups of people as they respond to an identical problem (such as male/female or immature/mature brain differences).

These research developments have sparked an immense interest in the development of a comprehensive brain theory that will be of the scientific magnitude of $E=MC^2$ in that it will spark a revolution in the brain sciences analogous to the revolution in the physical sciences that followed Albert Einstein's relativity theories at the beginning of the twentieth century. Powerful new theories tend to escalate the quality and quantity of our knowledge in an area. It's difficult to predict when such a definitive brain theory might emerge, but it inevitably will lead to a new major educational theory early in the twenty-first century that will transform educational thought and practice. The twentieth century has been the century for physics. The twenty-first century will be the century for brain/body biology—our century.

COMPUTER TECHNOLOGY

A related electronics explosion is occurring in computer technology, which has gone through three distinct revolutions within one human generation: from mainframe computer to personal computer to Internet. Computer technology has been important to the escalation of brain research because it takes powerful computers to quickly analyze and report the vast amount of information that a brain constantly processes. Similarly, brain research advances computer technology in the development of intelligent systems that better complement our cognitive systems.

The recent development of relatively inexpensive, powerful portable computers is fundamentally changing many areas of human life, and especially those that require rapid and precise verbal and/or numerical computations. Regrettably, schools have lagged in the use of computerized technologies. The school, alas, is the last pencil-driven institution in our society.

EDUCATIONAL CHALLENGES

As we discover more about the capabilities and limitations of brains and computers, educators will need to explore how best to approach instructional tasks that we historically have assigned to brains because we had no real processing options (for example, a pencil doesn't have a spell checker) or that we taught via a currently much more cumbersome technology (such as paper-and-pencil arithmetic computation). Further, computerized research technologies now available to elementary students often contain relevant musical and filmed information that is impossible to include in print encyclopedias.

Our profession is relatively unacquainted with brain research and computer technology, and that's a large part of the problem of incorporating them into educational policy and practice. Our profession is grounded principally in the social and behavioral sciences— we teach student in classroom-sized groups—and the social and behavioral sciences provide useful information on how to work effectively with groups of brains, even if they don't understand how one brain works. Further, the cognitive sciences only recently have begun to solve the teaching/learning problems that have long mystified us, and inexpensive portable computer technologies, such as laptop computers and pocket-sized calculators, likewise have emerged relatively recently.

We thus have no reason to apologize for what we did, but we now have massive curricular reconstruction and staff-development problems. We shouldn't necessarily abandon our social and behavioral sciences roots or the print and paper/pencil technologies we've depended on. Rather, we now also must understand and incorporate the biological substrate of the educative process and comfortably use the marvelous new information technologies that are available to us.

It's a monumental task. This book will help you to begin that process. It focuses on four especially significant areas: the nature of the current cognitive science revolution, the emerging importance of emotion in cognition, the biological substrate of intelligence, and the emerging relationship between our brains and computers in computational thought processes. The book includes fourteen recent articles that address various elements of these issues and recommended reading lists of the best recently published nontechnical books in each field—books that will get you into a deeper exploration of the specific issues that interest you. (And a bit of advice here: this is such a rapidly developing field that, in general, you should focus your reading on materials published within the past five years.) In addition, mass circulation magazines include articles about developments as they occur, and this book includes four such articles. These cognitive/computer revolutions interest many people, and so mass media tend to provide useful nontechnical reports of related developments.

It would be nice if someone could wave a magic wand and all educators suddenly would understand complex cognitive science terminology and systems, could easily debug all computer glitches, and would know the correct solution to the monumental challenges our profession now faces.

Alas, there's no quick fix. You'll have to begin a serious personal self-study program if you haven't already done so. Don't consider it an onerous chore. We are in the midst of the two most significant revolutions in our profession's history, and it's marvelous to be an integral part of it. It's happening on our watch. We get to be present and involved at the beginning. It's an exciting challenge, and your commitment to this book signals that you're willing to take the challenge to become a leader in the transformation of our profession. Good for you! Don't stop now. Read on. And on and on and on, beyond this book.

Section 1

Education and the Current Cognitive Science Revolution

D NA was discovered in 1953. Thus, more than forty years ago, scientists understood the biology of genetics, but it has been only during the last decade of the twentieth century that most of the genetic engineering applications have occurred, with one such application, cloning, occuring only within the late 1990s.

Similarly, the road between brain theory, laboratory research, and practical applications will be much longer and more tortuous than most educators realize. Laboratory researchers can reduce variables and focus entirely on the specific cognitive system they are studying. For example, a researcher attempting to identify a specific element of the attention system can eliminate all extraneous sounds, sights, and smells that might distract the experimental subject and thus compromise the study. An educational researcher trying to study *attention* within a classroom faces a much more complicated situation in that it is almost impossible to similarly control the distractions. Further, ethical constraints limit the kind of research that one can conduct with children. Thus, difficult as it is for scientists to study the neurobiology of attention, educational researchers face an even more daunting task in discovering how best to regulate it so that it is biologically appropriate.

The two articles in this section discuss the problems our profession faces in its strong desire for immediate practical applications from scientific discovery. We are compassionate about the problems our students face, and we want to help them. Right now. We are frustrated when immediate solutions do not emerge. These articles describe the issues and suggest how educators might best proceed in the practical environment of a classroom.

Think of it this way: What are the practical applications of an infant? It is basically a wet, noisy pet, twenty years at best from a clear sense of how it will turn out. What we do with infants is observe them carefully and nurture them. We try out things such as music lessons and ball hitting, if we notice interest and ability, but we don't make wild promises about their accomplishments (except perhaps in holiday letters). As childhood merges into adolescence, real interests and abilities become clearer and then we invest more heavily and decisively in *practical applications.*

Similarly, the brain sciences are in reality still in their infancy (but growing rapidly). It's a time to put our energy into getting acquainted with this *infant* that will change our professional lives— to observe, explore, and nurture. Our discoveries about our children generally don't surprise us, because we've provided them with their *genes* and *jeans.* Similarly, many brain science discoveries won't surprise us either because we've been working with a room full of brains for a long time, and although we may not understand neural networks and neurochemicals, we do know a lot about how minds function. Call it folklore knowledge if you wish, but our professional instincts generally have served us well. It's a good beginning, but we now have to get beyond a folklore understanding of the brain.

On Using Knowledge About Our Brain: A Conversation with Bob Sylwester

by Ron Brandt

W*e're hearing a lot about the brain lately. There are books like your* A Celebration of Neurons *(1995), feature articles in popular magazines, conferences, and so on. What accounts for this sudden interest?*

People are intrigued by dramatic developments in research technology, the ability to "get inside" our brain and observe how it functions. Today, researchers can learn about blood flow, electromagnetic fields, and chemical composition of the brain without interfering with normal brain functioning. What's called functional MRI (magnetic resonance imaging) allows them to have subjects do something—like sing a song or do a math problem—and watch what parts of the brain "light up" on a computer screen. Until MRI became available, most brain research was done only with animal brains or on people who had brain damage.

And along with imaging there are other technologies, like high-powered electron microscopes.

Right. With them, you can work at the cellular level—see neurons and synapses and the connections among them. And computers help, too, because rather than study a person's actual brain you can study a computerized version of it. You can single out the serotonin system and see what the serotonin level is related to (for example, a new study says it's related to autism). You can compare male brains and female brains, or an aggressive person with a nonaggressive person, or a Republican with a Democrat (just joking). But all such group differences are now accessible.

For most of human history, the human brain was impenetrable; the skull got in the way. And even when you looked at a brain, you didn't know what you were seeing—100 billion neurons, plus 10 times as many glial cells (support cells). How many is 100 billion? Well, there are about 100,000 hairs on the average head, so that would be all the hairs on the heads of a million people—that's how many neurons you have in your brain. You can put 30,000 neurons into a space the size of a pinhead. Without modern technology, it was impossible to study the brain.

> In science, when there's a big technological breakthrough, researchers start working on questions that until now were unanswerable.

This whole field is very new, then.
Yes. Modern brain research began about 30 years ago with brain hemisphere studies. Roger Sperry worked with about two dozen people with epilepsy whose doctors had completely severed their corpus callosums. Today, if a person suffers from epilepsy, a surgeon can locate the problem in a particular part of the brain—maybe less than a cubic millimeter—and, using advanced technology, possibly excise just those few neurons that need to be removed.

There's another reason for interest in our brain. If you have brain scans and nothing else, all you have is pretty pictures. But with this new information, we've had a parallel boom in theory development. For example, William Calvin (1996) has identified what he thinks is the location and coding system of intelligent behavior—a horizontal wiring pattern in the top three layers of the cortex. If he's right, it could do for brain science what the discovery of DNA did for genetics.

With all this activity, do you expect a steady stream of new information about the brain in the years ahead?
Oh, yes. In science, when there's a big technological breakthrough, researchers start working on questions that until now were unanswerable. And as pieces of knowledge start coming in, they begin to see how things fit together. So eventually, we'll have the universal brain theory. We'll be able to deal with consciousness: how we know what we know and how we know we know it.

Naturally, educators are interested in all of this. They are looking for ways they can apply the new knowledge from brain research in their schools. What do you say?

Well, I think we've done it all along, but we didn't call it brain research. If you're a teacher, you're dealing every day with about 100 pounds of brain tissue floating several feet above the classroom floor. Over a 20- or 30-year career, watching how those brains react, what they like to do, what they do easily and what with great difficulty, you're going to try to adapt your procedures to what works with brains. So, at that level, teachers have always been brain researchers.

> **If you're a teacher, you're dealing every day with about 100 pounds of brain tissue floating several feet above the classroom floor.**

We've known, for example, how long a lesson should be to hold student interest. We've known that more boys have trouble with reading and writing than do girls, and that young children can pick up a foreign language more easily than adults can. But we didn't have a biological substrate for that. Now, we're beginning to add this biological dimension that helps us understand why these things are true.

You know, people were successfully breeding dogs and horses long before DNA was discovered 40 years ago. It's taken 40 years to move from animal breeding to genetic engineering. So it took a while to find practical applications of this monumental discovery.

So what about practical applications of neuroscience?

We must take the time and effort to learn all we can about our brain—then figure out what to do about it. We teachers never really knew what was going on in those kids' brains. Now we have a chance to get beyond compassion and frustration. But first we have to really understand.

What is brain-compatible teaching?

I'm hesitant to use that term because it seems too pat. It seems to negate everything positive that teachers have been trying to do in the past. When the neurosciences come up with a discovery, it usually isn't a big surprise to most educators. For example, teachers have long encouraged students to find patterns and connections in what they've learned, but new knowledge about our brain may help us discover new ways to help students expand their knowledge. And the best teachers know that kids learn more readily when they are emotionally involved in the lesson because emotion drives attention, which drives learning and memory. It's biologically impossible to learn anything that you're not paying attention to; the attentional mechanism drives the whole learning and memory process. Teachers know that emotion is important; they just don't always know what to do about it.

The point is that teachers need to study many things—biology, anthropology, psychology, and other subjects—and make their own discoveries about improving instruction.

Let's take attention research, for example. For very good reasons, our brain evolved to be good at sizing things up quickly and acting on the basis of limited information. This has big survival value, because it keeps you from being eaten by predators. You don't need to know how old they are and whether they're male or female; you just get out of there as quickly as you can. But because of this tendency of our brains to make quick judgments, we go through life jumping to conclusions, making a mess of things, and then having to apologize.

So we're very good at rapidly sizing things up and acting on limited information, but we're not so good at the reverse—anything that requires sustained attention and precision, like worksheets. That doesn't mean worksheets are bad; it depends on how you're using them. But some are clearly not used appropriately.

I've heard you say that our profession needs to move from dependence on social science to greater emphasis on biology. What do you have in mind?

Throughout history, educators have worked with brains—with limited information on how brains work. In this century, we have turned to the social scientists, who don't know about one brain but do know about bunches of them. So our professional education has focused on negotiating behavior with a group of kids, on allocating energy and resources.

Now, the social scientists could be compassionate about something like dyslexia; they could tell what percentage of the population would have the problem, but they couldn't solve it. Biologists look at underlying causes; they can help us understand what dyslexia is. The problem is that biologists deal with neurons and synapses and blood and tissue, which most educators didn't study in their professional preparation.

But in the years ahead, they will?

They'll have to. Teacher education programs will have to change. I can't imagine a person preparing to become a teacher these days without having access to cognitive science.

What would you emphasize if you were teaching future teachers?

The first thing would be that we are basically a social species. We are born with an immature brain and have a long childhood, so we have to depend on other people to take care of us in childhood. The marvelous thing about our maturation process is that our individual brains develop very differently—just like the files individuals may later create in their computers. Our brains develop in their own way, which lends credence to the idea of multiple intelligences and specialization. When we think about implications of our social brain, we see that everybody in a community must know how to do some things, such as communicate, but not everyone has to be able to repair automobiles.

> I can't imagine a person preparing to become a teacher these days without having access to cognitive science.

Another obvious implication is the need to consider whether a particular learning task is individually oriented or socially oriented. It's foolish and wasteful to teach something to individuals if it's really a socially oriented behavior. I mentioned worksheets earlier. I saw a worksheet recently on which elementary students were supposed to list the five best qualities of a president—and hand it in with no discussion or feedback. Now, that's the kind of task we humans do more easily and naturally through discussion. It's not like a worksheet of multiplication problems, which is an individual task.

Another thing a biological approach can do for educators is change the way they think about education. For example, we talk about "higher order" and "lower order" as though one is much more important than the other. But it's really quite remarkable that we have the ability to remember a simple fact like where we're supposed to be at 12:30. If you can't remember the name of the restaurant where you're supposed to meet somebody, it may be lower thinking, but it's critical.

Another misconception is that the really important things are the hardest: Tasks that require a lot of energy and effort, like calculus, are the most significant. Biologically, that's just wrong. The way your brain looks at it, if it's important, it has to be a fail-safe opera-tion—like digital competence, the ability to pick things up. If it's re-ally important, you don't have to go to school to learn it; you can do it quickly and easily.

Why is it that the same kids who learned to speak their native language with no formal schooling—and who could have learned any language in the world the same way—have so much trouble learning to read and write? The answer scientists give is that reading and writing aren't nearly as critical to survival as is oral competency. That doesn't mean we should ignore the unnatural things, but it does mean that we sometimes get our priorities wrong when we talk about standards and rigor and so on. We need to remember that from a biological standpoint, importance and difficulty are not at all the same.

You've said that in the future, teachers will know more about the brain. In the meantime, what advice can you give today's educators?
First, as I said before, take the time to begin learning about this. Read books by educators and by the brain scientists themselves. Exciting new books are being published almost every week.

Second, think about how what you're learning applies to educa-tion—but broadly, not narrowly. We don't need catchy program titles. We do need to study and contemplate, discuss and explore. If something sounds like a good idea, try it. And don't worry too much about making exploratory mistakes. We have this marvelous student feedback system; when we try out inappropriate ideas on our stu-dents, they let us know.

Last, don't promise too much. You aren't going to be able to boost SAT scores with this knowledge; it's just too early for that. And many important brain properties, such as metaphor, compassion, and love, aren't measurable. By all means read and study. By all means try new ideas. But don't overpromise.

REFERENCES

Calvin, W. (1996). *How Brains Think: Evolving Intelligence Then and Now.* New York: Basic Books.

Sylwester, R. (1995). *A Celebration of Neurons: An Educator's Guide to the Human Brain.* Alexandria, Va.: ASCD.

Smart Brains

Neuroscientists explore the mystery of what makes us human

by Rebecca Jones

O h, the stories neuroscientists can tell. They tell of shrinking brains, blinded kittens, and children who have had hemispherectomies—half their brains removed   in an effort to control seizures.

They especially like to tell of a man known as H.M. Back in the 1950s, H.M. opted for surgery to stop the seizures that medication couldn't control. His medial temporal lobes, located near the bottom of his brain, were removed, and the seizures stopped. So did his ability to form a memory.

Now in his 60s, H.M. still has a normal IQ, can still carry on a conversation, and can still learn new things. He just can't remember anything that's happened in the 40 years since his surgery. (He has vivid memories of earlier years, though.) If someone shows him how to perform a task, he can do it until he is distracted. Then he immediately forgets everything he has learned; when he goes back to the task, he needs the instructions repeated.

What fascinates neuroscientists is that, although H.M. can't remember learning the task (or even meeting the person who spent hours or days working with him) from one distracted moment to the next, his performance on the task steadily improves at the same pace as someone who remembers the instructions. This oddity was scientists' first clue that the brain stores different kinds of memories in different locations.

From *The American School Board Journal,* November 1995, pp. 22–26. © 1995 by the National School Boards Association. All rights reserved. Reprinted with permission.

Other clues and discoveries have followed. The pace has been especially rapid in the last five or 10 years, as new technologies opened windows to the brain. Functional magnetic resonance imaging (MRI) and position emission tomography (PET) allow scientists to watch the blood flow to different parts of the brain, so they can see what areas are activated for the neural firings that mean connections are being made and learning is taking place. "We get to look inside the box," says Walter Schneider, senior scientist at the Learning Research and Development Center at the University of Pittsburgh.

> ... almost every major university now has teams, often composed of interdisciplinary scientists, working on brain research.

What scientists see is so intriguing, with a potential so promising, that almost every major university now has teams, often composed of interdisciplinary scientists, working on brain research. Even the none-too-cerebral U.S. Congress has recognized the 1990s as the Decade of the Brain—although it's not clear what that declaration means because brain scientists complain, like everyone else, that they aren't getting the funding they need. At least brain scientists know they have our attention and respect.

LOOKING FOR THE PAYOFF

Amidst all the hoopla, we should be forgiven if we expect something practical to come of this for schools: some advice, perhaps, on how to make young brains more receptive to learning and less susceptible to violence. But neuroscientists say they are at the beginning of their scientific journey and are in no position to offer advice to educators.

That doesn't mean advice is unavailable. Many books, articles, and lectures cite brain research as the reasoning behind advice that is sometimes sound and sometimes terrible. Most of the so-called brain research making its rounds among educators these days is based on studies—or theories—about how children learn. That's a fine field of study, made honorable by the likes of John Dewey and Howard Gardner, but it's totally separate, for now, from what neuroscientists are learning about the biochemistry of learning.

Sometimes, in fact, theories credited to brain research run counter to what scientists are finding inside the skull. One popular theory, for instance, tells teachers to create "brain-compatible classrooms" by establishing nonthreatening environments where children feel safe to learn. The nonthreatening classrooms sound like a good idea to neuroscientists, but they're puzzled by the link to brain research. If anything, their research indicates that lessons learned under stress would be better remembered than ones learned in a nonthreatening environment. The reason, according to psychiatrist Arnold Scheibel, lies in the reticular core, a network of nerves and fibers located in the brain stem. "It's a very primitive area," says Scheibel, who stepped down last summer as director of UCLA's Brain Research Institute, "and one of its most important roles is to make quick-and-dirty estimates as to whether input is strange and unexpected or dangerous. It is the reticular core, apparently, that triggers the upper part of the brain to be the most active" and lay down new connections. The reticular core is probably responsible for the flashbacks that haunt victims after trauma.

> . . . it will be at least 25 years before the benefits of brain research reach the classroom.

Another popular theory purportedly ascribed to brain research says teachers should explain concepts rather than require memorization. But neuroscientists say repetition is what produces the physiological changes necessary for learning. "If you want to know six times nine is 54, just brute, rote memorization might be the best way to get that information in," says Steven Petersen, a brain-imaging researcher at Washington University's School of Medicine in St. Louis.

Nobody is suggesting that children be tortured into repeating their multiplication tables or spitting back facts about the Civil War. Scientists insist it's far too soon to reach any conclusions from brain research that might change the way a school or a curriculum is designed. John Bruer, president of the James S. McDonnell Foundation that funds research in cognitive neuroscience, figures it will be at least 25 years before the benefits of brain research reach the classroom. "I'm rather skeptical of what the implications are going to be for my kids, who are in the third and fourth grades right now, or even for my grandkids," he says.

WHAT'S COMING SOON

The first benefits of brain research seem pledged to the medical profession. *Delivering Results: A Progress Report on Brain Research,* published by the Charles A. Dana Alliance for Brain Initiatives earlier this year, describes new drugs and therapies for Alzheimer's disease, multiple sclerosis, cocaine addiction, cerebral palsy, Parkinson's disease, and other maladies—but offers nothing to children with growing minds.

"What can brain scientists tell educators?" asks Susan Fitzpatrick, a neuroscientist at the McDonnell Foundation. "Not a heck of a lot."

The reason, she says, is that scientists are only beginning to learn about the physiology of learning: "Anything that people would say right now has a good chance of not being true two years from now because the understanding is so rudimentary and people are looking at things at such a simplistic level."

> Petersen suspects the early conclusions about the differences between male and female thought processes might also be wrong.

Already some intriguing ideas have come and gone—in scientific circles, if not elsewhere. Many educators and pop psychologists still cling to the old left-brain/right-brain theory that claims people use one side of their brains for analytical thinking and the other for creativity. And others still believe the notion that a person uses only 10 percent of his or her brain.

Misconceptions like these have led to curriculum plans that "are wrong-headed at best," says Washington University's Steven Petersen, an associate professor of neurology and neurosurgery. Like many brain scientists, he is especially concerned about stereotypes and teaching techniques based on the idea that children favor one side of the brain over the other. Imaging studies show "all people use all of their brain," he says: "The right-brained kids aren't turning off their left brains, and the left-brained kids aren't turning off their right brains. I know scientists who are amazingly linear and amazingly creative. Which 'brain' are they? I also know people who are unlinear and uncreative. Do they not use their brains at all?"

Petersen suspects the early conclusions about the differences between male and female thought processes might also be wrong. The popular conclusion today—essentially that, as the best-seller says, "men are from Mars and women are from Venus"—is based on imaging studies that showed men and women use different regions of the brain to recognize rhyming words. The differences, Petersen thinks, might have more to do with the different tactics the subjects used than with functional differences in their brains. Perhaps women tend to sound out words, for instance, while men look for visual signs of rhyming. "It just seems so unlikely that one species has developed two different ways of handling that unbelievably complicated system of language," Petersen says.

> ... they [scientists] agree that the biochemistry of learning remains, for the most part, a mystery.

Other scientists might disagree with Petersen's thoughts about that specific study, but they agree that the biochemistry of learning remains, for the most part, a mystery. "There is an entire fundamental groundwork that has to be laid so we can understand the basic mechanisms," says Fitzpatrick.

A SLAB OF MEAT

Some scientists describe the brain as a 3-pound slab of meat, about one-half meter wide and one-half meter long. It "gets stuffed into a head that's only about 15 centimeters across," says researcher Schneider, so "it gets crumpled rather severely." As one of the early geographers mapping out the functions of the brain, Schneider "uncrumples" MRI images of the brains on a computer screen to create maps so detailed that they reveal 1,000 different regions, each about the size of a pencil tip and each associated with a different function. (Another way to understand that, he says, is to imagine an uncrumpled brain stretched out to the size of a football field that is covered with sheets of typing paper laid end-to-end; each piece of paper represents a different brain function.)

Different types of learning take place, as H.M.'s case would suggest, on different parts of the map. At Washington University, Steven Petersen is on a research team that is studying the images of brains trying to figure out mazes on computer screens. Before that, the researchers studied images of brains that were reading nouns and thinking of verbs—reading "cake," for instance, and thinking of "eat." They found "there is one set of brain regions that you can use for automatic tasks, like simple word reading, and another set of brain regions that you use when you're presented with a novel situation, like having to come up with a verb for a noun," Petersen says.

The brain seems to use one set of "scaffolding" to handle new information and another set of scaffolding to store the old. "The first time you're handed a novel situation, your brain has to set up a way of handling the situation," Petersen says. When the situation comes up again, "the brain thinks, 'OK, I'm going to have to deal with this many times. I want to make this much more efficient than having to build up this new scaffolding every time.'"

Petersen realizes they are working on the very basics of intellectual functioning, and he calls the connection between brain research and education "a bridge too far to cross." Still, he wonders where his research might lead. Maybe it will help explain the different forms that a problem like dyslexia can take. Children with learning disabilities "could have trouble setting up the scaffolding in the first place, they could have trouble storing the program, they could have trouble accessing the stored program," or they could have any combination of those problems, he says.

Different varieties of learning disabilities obviously require different types of intervention—and not all of the interventions involve teaching strategies.

Both research and practical experience have shown that many forms of dyslexia exist. Some children's reading problems are rooted in "auditory timing errors" that cause them to "miss the natural breaks that we hear in our native language," says neuroscientist Fitzpatrick; others have trouble with visual input. Similarly, scientists are identifying many varieties of attention deficit disorder. "Some children have trouble fixating, and others have trouble breaking their attention," Fitzpatrick says, which would make it hard for them to move from word to word as they read.

Different varieties of learning disabilities obviously require different types of intervention—and not all of the interventions involve teaching strategies. Brain research has led to the development of eyeglasses, for instance, that correct the input for children with some visual dyslexias. "You need to be able to diagnose these problems properly," Fitzpatrick says, which means MRIs, PET scans, and electroencephalograms (EEGs) probably will be needed for children with learning disabilities. (Those tests aren't cheap—the bill for having a functional MRI now runs between $500 and $1,000—so some researchers warn that school boards might expect pressure to foot some big bills in the future.)

OTHER EARLY IMPLICATIONS

Despite their constant disclaimers about the applicability of current research to schools today, scientists acknowledge several findings that do seem to have clear implications for education:

- **The importance of early learning opportunities for the very young.** The brain remains plastic—that is, it retains the ability to make new neural connections—throughout life, but it is most plastic in the first five or six years of life. And certain connections must be made at certain times, or the opportunity is lost forever. David Hubel and Torsten Wiesel received a Nobel prize for research that demonstrated the necessity of early neural connections in the development of eyesight in cats. They put eyepatches over kittens' eyes shortly after birth. When they removed the patches several weeks later, they found the kittens were blind in that eye. The eye structure was fine, but the proper connections to the brain had not been made, so the cats never did develop vision in those once-patched eyes.

Similar phenomena have been reported in humans. Earlier this year, ABC's "PrimeTime Live" told of a woman who could not hear from birth but didn't receive hearing aids until she was 31. Again, the early deprivation prevented the proper connections from being made; even now, after 13 years of intense therapy, her speech is often garbled.

That woman's experience emphasizes what other research has found: The early years in a child's life are critical for language development—a fact that makes elementary school the best time to offer second, third, and fourth languages. "Neuroscientists know quite easily that if you want to learn a second language, you should do it before puberty," says Fitzpatrick. "The brain plasticity for language changes around that time"—so introductory language classes in high schools might be too late for many of the students who want to speak other languages fluently.

- **The connections between music and abstract reasoning.** The genius of young musical prodigies has long made scientists wonder about the connections between brain waves and music. In years of research that seem both dogged and whimsical, physicists at the University of California at Irvine developed mathematical models for the neural firing patterns associated with brain functions, then mapped musical pitches onto these patterns. They found the higher brain functions, when set to music, sounded like a Mozart sonata. So psychologist Frances Rauscher began a study that measured the effects of music lessons on 3-year-olds. She found children who received keyboarding and singing lessons scored between eight and 10 points higher on IQ tests that measured their spatial-temporal skills—the reasoning skills that are so important in understanding math and engineering concepts. (In a separate study, she found college students scored higher on spatial-temporal tests immediately after listening to 10 minutes of a Mozart sonata.)

The research continues at the university's Center for the Neurobiology of Learning and Memory in Irvine, where physicist Gordon Shaw expects the studies to continue with children in the early grades. But Rauscher has moved on to a new position at the University of Wisconsin at Oshkosh, where one of her first appointments was to speak with teachers and school board members about the importance of music lessons. "I do whatever I can to get the word out," she says. "Now that we know music has benefits to intelligence, it's a disservice not to provide [children] with the best opportunities we can."

• **The importance of good nutrition.** Everyone knows hunger can be a terrible barrier to learning. But research shows the need for good nutrition begins long before a child enters school—or is even born. When psychiatrist Scheibel was in Kenya with his wife, neurobiologist Marian Diamond, they both wondered about the connection between the glassy-eyed children they saw on the street and the practice of some Kenyan women to limit food intake during pregnancy in hopes of making childbirth easier. After returning to her lab at the University of California at Berkeley, Diamond experimented with limiting food to pregnant rats. "The little ratlets showed much smaller brain structure and a great deal less ability" to learn, says Scheibel. When Diamond gave the baby rats more food, "they were able to bring back some, but never all, of brain size."

The lesson to Scheibel is clear: We need to improve nutrition for pregnant women. "We have lost a couple of generations—lost them, in the sense that they are below their potential," he says. "If we can somehow educate now the group that will become pregnant in the next five or 10 years," we might be able to improve the educational prospects of future generations.

NOTHING NEW?

These ideas—teaching children when they're young, enriching their lives with music, and feeding them well—are certainly not startling. Maybe we're expecting too much of brain science. Or maybe we're not appreciating ourselves enough.

When the McDonnell Foundation, the Dana Alliance, the Brain Research Institute, and other organizations schedule workshops and conferences to bring science and education together, the scientists usually stand at the podium while the educators take notes. But some neuroscientists see something wrong with that picture. Brain research is at such a rudimentary level, says Susan Fitzpatrick, that "I think the flow of information should be going the other way. Educators probably have a lot of interesting observations that brain scientists could use."

RECOMMENDED READINGS

Pinker, Steven. *How the Mind Works.* New York: Norton, 1997. Written by a leading cognitive scientist, this is a very important, absolutely fascinating, far-reaching, often humorous synthesis of the emergence of the mind from the brain. It's a good introduction to the rapidly emerging field of evolutionary psychology and to the important perspectives of human nature that recently have emerged from it. Thoughtful and thought provoking, it's a 600-page delight.

Posner, Michael, and Marcus Raichle. *Images of Mind.* New York: W. H. Freeman, 1996. Two leading researchers in the field have collaborated on the best current book on brain imaging technology for general readers. Part of the Scientific American Library series, it contains a wealth of useful information on diagnostic imaging technology that is expected to become available to educators in the very near future. Many libraries carry the Scientific American Library series.

Davis, Joel. *Mapping the Mind: The Secrets of the Human Brain and How It Works.* Secaucus, NJ: Carol Publishing Group, 1997.

Greenfield, Susan. *The Human Brain: A Guided Tour.* New York: Basic Books, 1997.

Kotulak, Ron. *Inside the Brain: Revolutionary Discoveries of How the Mind Works.* Kansas City, MO: Andrews and McMeel, 1996.

Sylwester, Robert. *A Celebration of Neurons: An Educator's Guide to the Human Brain.* Alexandria, VA: Association for Supervision and Curriculum Development, 1995.

These are four very easily read introductory books for educators who want to know how the brain and its cognitive systems function but are fearful of technological terminology and complicated explanations. All four books include ample explanatory material that teachers easily can use with their students.

The Emergence and Importance of Emotion

E motion is much more difficult to study than reason or logic. Reason and logic are conscious and factual and thus lend themselves easily to verbal report. Emotion is unconscious and emerges as bodily states and feelings that don't easily lend themselves to verbal report. For example, we can easily report precise factual information on someone we love (such as "She's 5'6""), but our language of love is vague at best (for example, "She's the light of my life"). It thus has been very difficult to scientifically study our emotional lives.

Scientists recently have made major advances in their ability to study emotion, and the result is an explosion of new information. Emotion is our body/brain's unconscious system for alerting itself to dangers and opportunities. Feelings are the conscious awareness of important unconscious emotional signals. Emotion thus drives attention, which drives learning, memory, problem solving, and just about everything else we do. It's biologically impossible to learn something we're not attending to, and it's foolish to attend to something that's emotionally meaningless. The school's longstanding relative disinterest in exploring ways of incorporating emotion into the curriculum, although understandable, consequently has been a disaster. We are now decades behind in seriously exploring how best to do it.

Daniel Goleman is the cognitive/behavioral science writer for the *New York Times,* and as such he frequently reports the dramatic advances of emotion research. His recent excellent book-length synthesis of this research, *Emotional Intelligence,* introduced many educators to the important educational challenge that our profession had virtually ignored. It further suggested that it is possible for schools to do much to enhance the emotional lives of students. The first article in this section provides a good synthesis of his book (and hopefully will encourage you to read the entire book if you haven't already done so). The list of recommended readings suggests two very recent books that go even further in proposing practical applications of emotion research.

The second article, "How Emotions Affect Learning," provides a nontechnical introduction to the neurobiology of our emotional system. Knowing how the system works is the first step on the way to exploring practical ways of better incorporating emotion into school life.

Two emotionally related and educationally significant human properties are the development of our personal and social identities—Who am I? and Who are these people around me? Howard Gardner's theory of multiple intelligences refers to these as intrapersonal intelligence and interpersonal intelligence. We're a social species, and so it's important both to strive and compete and to cooperate and collaborate.

The final two articles in this section provide nontechnical background information on recent studies of neurotransmitter and hormonal systems (principally serotonin and oxytocin) that appear to play major roles in regulating our personal and social identities. Emotion is a fascinating emerging scientific story with many intriguing applications to educational practice.

On Emotional Intelligence: A Conversation with Daniel Goleman

by John O'Neil

Traditional conceptions of intelligence focus on cognitive skills and knowledge. You've investigated the idea of "emotional intelligence." What do you mean by that term?

Emotional intelligence is a different way of being smart. It includes knowing what your feelings are and using your feelings to make good decisions in life. It's being able to manage distressing moods well and control impulses. It's being motivated and remaining hopeful and optimistic when you have setbacks in working toward goals. It's empathy; knowing what the people around you are feeling. And it's social skill—getting along well with other people, managing emotions in relationships, being able to persuade or lead others.

And you contend that emotional intelligence is just as important as the more familiar concept of IQ?

Both types of intelligence are important, but they're important in different ways. IQ contributes, at best, about 20 percent to the factors that determine life success. That leaves 80 percent to everything else. There are many ways in which your destiny in life depends on having the skills that make up emotional intelligence.

From *Educational Leadership*, September 1996, pp. 6–11. © 1996 by the Association for Supervision and Curriculum Development. All rights reserved. Reprinted with permission.

Has research shown such a correlation?

Yes. For example, boys who are very impulsive, who are always getting in trouble in 2nd grade, are six to eight times more likely than other kids to commit crimes and be violent in their teen years. Sixth grade girls who confuse feelings of anxiety and anger, boredom, and hunger are the ones most likely to develop eating disorders in adolescence. What these girls lack is an awareness of what they are feeling; they're confused about what this feeling is and what it's called. So specific deficits in these skills can get a person in trouble, particularly a child who is growing into adulthood. On the other side, having these abilities can help you immensely in life; they affect everything from whether your marriage is going to last to how well you do on the job.

There's also a relationship between these emotional skills and academic success, isn't there?

Absolutely. It's not too surprising, really. We know that skills such as being able to resist impulsivity, or to delay gratification in pursuit of a long-term goal, are helpful in the academic arena.

Your book describes some fascinating findings from the "marshmallow" study at Stanford.

Right. Preschool kids were brought in one by one to a room and had a marshmallow put in front of them. They were told they could eat the marshmallow now, but if they delayed eating it until the researcher came back from running an errand, they could have two marshmallows. About one-third of them grabbed the single marshmallow right away while some waited a little longer, and about one-third were able to wait 15 or 20 minutes for the researcher to return.

When the researchers tracked down the children 14 years later, they found this test was an amazing predictor of how they did in school. The kids who waited were more emotionally stable, better liked by their teachers and their peers, and still able to delay gratification in pursuit of their goals. The ones who grabbed were emotionally unstable, they fell apart under stress, they were more irritable, more likely to pick fights, not as well liked, and still not able to delay gratification. But the most powerful finding was that the ones who waited scored an average of 210 points higher on the SAT.

Was that because their emotional habits were more conducive to studying, sticking with a task and thinking that it would eventually pay off?

That's part of it. Obviously, a child who can stick with a task can do his homework or can finish an assignment much better than a child who is distracted and goes off and does something else.

There's another factor, too: the physiology of the brain and the relationship between the emotional brain and the brain's executive areas. The prefrontal lobes just behind the forehead are where working memory resides. Working memory is what you are paying attention to at any given point. So everything you are mulling over, making a decision about, or are learning, is at first in working memory. All learning is in working memory. And the emotional centers that control moods like anxiety or anger have very strong connections to the prefrontal areas. So if a child is chronically anxious or angry or upset in some way, he experiences that as intruding thoughts. He can't keep his mind off the thing he is worried about.

> ... children whose emotional lives are more under control and better managed are able to learn more.

Now working memory has a limited attention capacity. So, to the extent that it is occupied by these intrusive thoughts, it shrinks what's available in working memory to think about what you are trying to learn.

Is that what's occurring when someone has "test anxiety"?

Yes, test anxiety is a very good example. You can think of nothing else except the fact that you may fail. It becomes a self-fulfilling prophecy, because your working memory cannot manage both the extreme anxiety and the demands for retrieving the information that would help you pass. So I think that's why we find that children whose emotional lives are more under control and better managed are able to learn more.

We all know people who have a lot of self-insight, or who are virtuosos in social situations. But are those kinds of personality traits something that people are born with, or can everyone be helped to develop them?

The good news about emotional intelligence is that it is virtually all learned. Even though newborn children differ in terms of their temperament, for example, they are highly malleable.

The best data on this come from Jerome Kagan, who studied shy kids. He found that you can identify a tendency toward shyness within the first two weeks of life, by looking at how much an infant startles to a noise or whether they are likely to shy away from stimulating, new, novel, uncertain experiences. He followed kids from birth into childhood and teenage years and found that this is a remarkable predictor of shyness.

> So if a child learns to manage his anger well, or learns to calm or soothe himself, or to be empathic, that's a lifelong strength.

But he also discovered that a subgroup of children whose newborn behaviors suggested that they would be shy turned out not to be. Kagan found that the parents of this group treated them differently. Instead of catering to the children's shyness and protecting them from the world, these parents pushed them a bit into challenging situations; you know, meet a new kid, let's go to this new place. Not in a way that overwhelmed them but in a way that gave them the continued experience of mastering something new. And by the time they got to kindergarten, those kids weren't shy. They weren't the most extroverted, but they weren't inordinately shy either.

What's the significance of these findings?

Well, they suggest something that, in theory, we've known all along: the brain is enormously malleable during childhood. The brain's regulatory centers for emotional response are among the last parts to become anatomically mature. They continue to grow into adolescence.

This is vitally important, because we're finding that the repeated emotional lessons of a child's life literally shape the brain circuits for that response. So if a child learns to manage his anger well, or learns to calm or soothe himself, or to be empathic, that's a lifelong strength. That's why it's so critical that we help children develop the skills of emotional intelligence.

What about children who learn the wrong *emotional responses from early on; who come from abusive homes, for example. Can they relearn emotional skills or do the initial strategies become "hard wired" in the brain?*

It's harder, but the sooner we begin to teach children appropriate emotional responses the sooner these responses can become a part of their repertoire.

A child may have learned that when you get mad, you yell and you hit. Someone has to help these children learn an alternative response that becomes stronger than the initial one. So instead of yelling and hitting, the child will stop, calm down, think before she acts, and so on.

Again, the good news about childhood is that it's a wonderful palette to work with. It may look like it's been painted on, but you can keep painting and eventually children can learn healthier emotional responses. The literature on resilient children, those who have grown up in the worst circumstances and yet thrived, shows that what made the difference wasn't the terrible circumstance of their chaotic home life, but the fact that one caring adult really got involved in their lives and helped them out. And oftentimes that person is a teacher.

Before talking about what schools can do to foster emotional intelligence, what can you say about the current state of the emotional well-being of children?

Childhood is harder than it used to be; we've got data on that. For example, in the last 20 years or so the rate of teen homicide has quadrupled and teen suicide tripled, and forcible rape among teens has doubled. Those are the headline-making statistics.

But there are other more subtle indicators of a growing general emotional malaise among children. Thomas Achenbach at the University of Vermont studied a random sample of American kids in the mid-70s and a comparable sample in the late '80s. He had them rated by their parents and teachers and found that, across the board, American kids on average had a growing deficit in these emotional skills. They had gone down on 40 indicators of emotional well-being, which is very alarming. This doesn't mean there aren't great kids, but on average kids were more impulsive, more disobedient, more angry, more lonely, more depressed, more anxious, and so on.

Let's face it: childhood has changed, and not necessarily in ways that anyone intended. The state of the economy now demands that parents work much harder and longer than they had to, so they have less discretionary time to spend with their kids than their own parents had with them. More families live in neighborhoods where they're scared about the kids even playing down the street, let alone going into a neighbor's house. And kids are spending more time glued to a TV or in front of a computer, away from other children or adults. And most of the emotional skills I've discussed aren't learned on your own, they're learned through your interaction with other children and adults. That's why the emphasis on computers concerns me, helpful as they can be. More time with computers and TV means less time with other people. The changes in families are another reason I think it's vital that schools begin to teach these emotional skills, to promote "emotional literacy."

You're familiar with schools that have been trying to teach emotional literacy. How are they doing this?

A good example is the program developed in the New Haven schools, which goes from 1st through 12th grade and is developmentally appropriate. The program addresses all the skills I mentioned before, like empathy, how to calm yourself down when you are feeling anxious, and so on. In some grades, lessons in emotional intelligence are taught as a separate topic three times a week. In other grades it's part of courses such as health, even math or study skills. And all the teachers are familiar with the ideas and look for opportunities to teach them. So whenever a child is upset, it's an opportunity to make sure that they learn something from that experience that will help them.

In New Haven, they also use techniques that make healthy emotional responses a pervasive part on the school culture or environment. For example, a school I recently visited had a "stoplight" poster on the wall of every room. It indicates to kids that whenever you are distressed or upset or you have a problem, red light—stop, calm down, and think before you act. Yellow light—think about a number of different things you could do and what the consequences will be. Green light—pick the best one and try it out. Now that's a wonderful lesson in impulse control, in soothing yourself, and in making the distinction between having the feeling and what you do, how you act when you have the feeling. These are crucial lessons and kids are really learning them.

That's encouraging, because one of the trends that worries educators is that students seem to be more impulsive, more prone to act without thinking about the consequences.

I've taken aside 7th graders in New Haven and said, "Look, I know they teach you this stuff, but does it really make any difference to you?" And they all have stories to tell about how they're using these skills in their lives.

In the culture of adolescents in New Haven, if someone "disses" you, you have to fight them; it's the code. But I talked to this kid, and he said: "You know, this guy was dissing my sneaks, and you know what I did? I told him I didn't agree with him. I like my shoes. And then I walked away." Well, that's revolutionary, and what's happening is that children are expanding their emotional repertoire in some healthy ways.

> **. . . the decline in emotional well-being holds true for all groups of kids, from wealthy areas and poor ones.**

What are they finding in terms of results?

Well, it works. They've found that students are better able to control their impulses, they've improved their behavior, they have better conflict-resolution skills and skills in handling interpersonal problems. That's consistent with what's happening in other programs aimed at emotional literacy.

It seems important that this emotional literacy curriculum is a schoolwide effort; it's not just isolating the kids who appear to have the worst emotional problems.

Ghettoizing is the wrong approach. For one thing, the decline in emotional well-being holds true for all groups of kids, from wealthy areas and poor ones. These lessons are not just for so-called problem kids.

The public appears to be very skeptical these days about curriculums that address social issues, or that ask kids to work on their emotions instead of on their reading and math. Isn't that a major obstacle to broader application of these ideas by schools?

Actually I've encountered the reverse. Parents and teachers are very interested in bringing this sort of curriculum into the schools, because they see that children need it. When they understand that you can do this without taking any time from the basics—which they've been able to do in New Haven—they're very supportive. It just makes good sense.

How Emotions Affect Learning

by Robert Sylwester

New developments in cognitive science are unraveling the mysteries of emotions; the findings have much to teach us about how students do—or do not—learn.

John Dewey began this century with an eloquent plea for the education of the *whole child*. If we get around to that kind of education by the end of the century, emotion research may well provide the catalyst we need.

Our profession pays lip service to the whole student, but school activities tend to focus on measurable rational qualities. We measure spelling accuracy, not emotional well-being. And when the budget gets tight, we cut curricular areas like the arts, expressive subjects that are difficult to measure.

We know emotion is important in education—it drives attention, which in turn drives learning and memory. But because we don't fully understand our emotional system, we don't know exactly how to regulate it in school, beyond defining too much or too little emotion as misbehavior. We have rarely incorporated emotion comfortably into the curriculum and classroom. Further, our profession hasn't fully addressed the important relationship between a stimulating and emotionally positive classroom experience and the overall health of both students and staff.

Recent developments in the cognitive sciences are unlocking the mysteries of how and where our body/brain processes emotion. This

From *Educational Leadership*, October 1994, pp. 60–65. © 1994 by the Association for Supervision and Curriculum Development. All rights reserved. Reprinted with permission.

unique melding of the biology and psychology of emotion promises to suggest powerful educational applications. Current emotion theory and research bring up more questions than answers. Still, educators should develop a basic understanding of the psychobiology of emotion to enable them to evaluate emerging educational applications.

Following is a basic introduction to the role our emotional system plays in learning, and the potential classroom applications of this research.

EMOTION AND REASON

Studies show that our emotional system is a complex, widely distributed, and error-prone system that defines our basic personality early in life, and is quite resistant to change.

Far more neural fibers project from our brain's emotional center into the logical/rational centers than the reverse, so emotion is often a more powerful determinant of our behavior than our brain's logical/rational processes. For example, purchasing a lottery ticket is an emotional, not a logical decision. (The odds are terrible, but where else can one buy three days of fantasy for $1?) Reason may override our emotions, but it rarely changes our *real* feelings about an issue. Our emotions allow us to bypass conscious deliberation of an issue, and thus to respond quickly based on almost innate general categorizations of incoming information. This may lead to irrational fears and foolish behavior: Often we don't consciously know why we feel as we do about something or someone.

Emotion, like color, exists along a continuum, with a wide range of gradations. We can easily identify many discrete emotions through their standard facial and auditory expressions, but the intensity and meaning of the emotion will vary among people and situations. Moreover, emotional context, like color hue, may affect our perception of emotion. To understand our constantly shifting emotional system and its effect on our capacity to learn, we must understand the system's two parts:

• the molecules (peptides) that carry emotional information, and

• the body and brain structures that activate and regulate emotions.

PEPTIDES: MOLECULAR MESSENGERS OF EMOTION

Traditionally, we've tended to think in terms of a body-brain split: Our brain regulates body functions, and our body provides support services for our brain. However, scientists now think in terms of an integrated body/brain system. Our emotional system is located principally in our brain, endocrine, and immune systems (which now are viewed as an integrated biochemical system), but it affects all other organs, such as our heart, lungs, and skin. Think of our emotions as the glue that integrates our body and brain, and peptide molecules as the physical manifestation of the process.

Peptide molecules are the messengers of our emotional system. We know a peptide molecule is a chain of amino acids that is shorter than a protein, and that more than 60 types are involved in emotions. But it's not yet clear how these molecules carry information, or even what that information is. Peptides developed within body/brain cells are called hormones and neuropeptides. (When similarly shaped molecules are developed outside our body, we call them drugs.)

Peptide molecules are the messengers of our emotional system.

To modulate our broad range of pleasure and pain, peptides travel throughout our body/brain via our neural networks, circulatory system, and air passages. They powerfully affect the decisions we make within the continuum of emotionally charged approaching and retreating behaviors, such as to drink-urinate, agree-disagree, and marry-divorce. In effect, the shifts in the body/brain levels of these molecules allocate our emotional energy—what we do, when we do it, and how much energy we expend.

At the cellular level, peptides synthesized within one cell attach to receptors on the outside of another, sparking increased or decreased cellular actions. If this occurs in large populations of cells, it can affect our emotional state. Cell division and protein synthesis are two such actions; both are heavily involved in the emotion-charged body changes during adolescence (Moyers 1992).

A peptide's message can vary in many different body/brain areas, just as a two-by-four can be used in many different ways in the construction of a house. In this way peptides are similar to many drugs. Alcohol, for example, can excite or sedate, depending on the drinker's emotional state and the amount ingested.

Cortisol and the endorphins are two good examples of peptide molecules that can affect students' behavior in the classroom. When our inability to fend off danger triggers a stress response, *cortisol*—a sort of all-purpose wonder drug—is released by our adrenal glands. It activates important body/brain defensive responses that vary with the nature and severity of the stressor. Developed eons ago when physical dangers most threatened our survival, our stress responses do not differentiate between physical and emotional danger.

> **Developed eons ago . . . our stress responses do not differentiate between physical and emotional danger.**

Because most contemporary stress results from emotional problems, these responses are often maladaptive. For example, a 2nd grader refuses to complete an arithmetic assignment. The irritated teacher's stress system inappropriately responds by releasing clotting elements into the blood, elevating cholesterol levels, depressing the immune system, tensing large muscles, increasing the blood pressure—and much more. It's a response that makes sense only if the recalcitrant student is also threatening with a knife or gun.

We pay a high price for chronic emotional stress. While low levels of cortisol produce the euphoria we feel when we're in control, high levels triggered by the stress response can induce the despair we often feel when we've failed. Moreover, chronic stress can also lead to a variety of circulatory, digestive, and immune disorders.

Chronic high cortisol levels can eventually destroy hippocampal neurons associated with learning and memory (Vincent 1990). Even short-term stress-related elevation of cortisol in the hippocampus can hinder our ability to distinguish between important and unimportant elements of a memorable event (Gazzaniga 1989). Thus, stressful school environments reduce the school's ability to carry out its principal mission.

More positively, *the endorphins* are a class of opiate peptides that modulate emotions within our pain-pleasure continuum; they reduce intense pain and increase euphoria. Endorphin levels can be elevated by exercise and by positive social contacts—hugging, music, a friend's supportive comments, among other things—thereby making us feel good about ourselves and our social environment (Levinthal 1988). A joyful classroom atmosphere that encourages such behaviors produces internal chemical responses in students that make them more apt to learn how to successfully solve problems in potentially stressful situations.

THE EMOTION REGULATORS

Although the endocrine and immune systems participate in processing our emotions, two interrelated brain systems share the regulating task:

1.   The finger size brain stem at the base of our brain and the limbic system structures surrounding it focus inward on our survival, emotional, and nurturing needs. The brain stem monitors involuntary activity, like breathing.

2.   The cerebral cortex, which regulates higher functions, addresses our interactions with the external world (Edelman 1992).

Regulator I: The Brain Stem and Limbic System

Extensively connected in looped circuits to body organs and systems, the brain stem and limbic system responds relatively slowly (from seconds to months) as it regulates basic body functions, cycles, and defenses. The system is loaded with peptide receptors. The *reticular formation* at the top of the brain stem integrates the amount and type of incoming sensory information into a general level of attention (Vincent 1990).

The *Limbic system,* composed of several small interconnected structures, *is our brain's principal regulator of emotion and plays important roles in processing memory.* This may explain why emotion is an important ingredient in many memories. The limbic system is powerful enough to override both rational thought and innate brain stem response patterns. In short, we tend to follow our feelings.

Memories formed during a specific emotional state tend to be easily recalled during a similar emotional state later on (Thayer 1989). For example, during an argument, we easily recall similar previous arguments. Thus, classroom simulations and role-playing activities enhance learning because they tie memories to the kinds of emotional contexts in which they will later be used.

The limbic system influences selection and classification of experiences that our brain stores in two forms of long-term memory—*procedural* (unconsciously processed skills, such as walking and talking) and *declarative* (conscious recall of facts, such as names and locations).

Limbic system structures that process emotion and memory are the amygdala complex, the hippocampus, and the thalamus and hypothalamus.

•   *Amygdala complex.* This is the principal limbic system structure involved in processing the emotional content of behavior and memory. It is composed of two small almond-shaped structures that connect our sensory-motor systems and autonomic nervous system (which regulates such survival function as breathing and circulation). The amygdala is also richly and reciprocally connected to most other brain areas. Its principal task is to filter and interpret sophisticated incoming sensory information in the context of our survival and emotional needs, and then help initiate appropriate responses. Thus, it influences both early sensory processing and higher levels of cognition (for example, ignoring the feel of a comfortable shoe, but responding to one with a tiny pebble in it).

•   *Hippocampus.* The amygdala adjoins the hippocampus, two finger-size structures that convert important short-term experiences into long-term declarative memories that are stored in the cortex. Think of the amygdala as processing the subjective feelings you associate with an event, and the hippocampus as processing the objective location, time, and actions that defined the event.

The brain's amygdala and the adjoining hippocampus can modulate the subjective and objective strength of a memory. Kandel and Kandel (1994) suggest that this helps explain, for example, the repressed memories of sexual abuse. The fearfulness of the abusive experience can lead to the release of certain substances (noradrenaline neurotransmitters) that strengthen the connections processing the emotional memory of the event. Conversely, the painfulness of the experience can lead to the release of *opiate endorphins* that weaken connections processing the conscious memory of the factual circumstances surrounding the event. Subsequently, the victim tends to avoid anything that triggers the fearful emotion, but doesn't consciously know why. Years later, a chance combination of similar characters, location, actions, and emotions may cause the strong emotional memory to trigger the recall of the weak factual memory of the original circumstances of the abuse.

•   *Thalamus and hypothalamus.* The walnut-size thalamus and adjoining pea-size hypothalamus are two other important related limbic system structures that help regulate our emotional life and physical safety.

The *thalamus* is our brain's initial relay center for incoming sensory information; it informs the rest of our brain about what's happening outside our body. The thalamus has direct connections to the amygdala, which permits it to send a vary rapid but factually limited report on a potential threat. This can trigger a quick, emotionally loaded (but perhaps also life-saving) behavior before we fully understand what's happening. And it is the mechanism that underlies many explosive emotional outbursts during a typical school day.

> **And it [the thalamus] is the mechanism that underlies many explosive emotional outbursts during a typical school day.**

The *hypothalamus* monitors our internal regulatory systems, informing our brain what's happening *inside* our body. When our brain has no solution to a threatening situation, the hypothalamus can activate a fight-flight stress response through its pituitary gland contacts with the endocrine gland system.

Pheromones are a newly discovered but poorly understood addition to our sensory system (although they've long been known to regulate many animal behaviors). They are molecules that are released into the air from the skin, entering a tiny vomeronasal organ in our nose, although they are not part of our sense of smell. This triggers neural activity in areas of the hypothalamus that regulate sexual behavior, levels of comfort, and self-confidence. The cheek area next to our nose is rich in pheromones, which may explain why we humans like to kiss while nuzzling our nose in that area.

Regulator II: The Cortex

The cerebral cortex, which occupies 85 percent of our brain's mass, is a large sheet of neural tissue that's deeply folded around the limbic system. It is organized into myriad highly interconnected and outwardly focused neural networks that respond very rapidly (in milliseconds to seconds) to various *space-time* demands. The system:

1. receives, categorizes, and interprets sensory information;
2. makes rational decisions; and
3. activates behavioral responses.

Space: Viewed from the unfolded top, the neocortex is divided into right and left hemispheres along a line that goes directly back from our nose. A simplified view of tasks of the two hemispheres suggests that they focus on different perspectives of an object or event. The right hemisphere *synthesizes* the background or contextual information (the forest); the left hemisphere *analyzes* the foreground information (a tree in the forest).

Although the research isn't conclusive on the roles the hemispheres (or lobes) play in emotion, some general patterns are apparent (Corballis 1991). The right hemisphere seems to play the more prominent role overall in processing emotions. It processes the important emotional content of faces, gestures, and language (intonation, volume)—*how* something was communicated; while the left hemisphere processes much of the objective content of language—*what* was said.

The right hemisphere processes the negative aspects that lead to withdrawal behaviors (for example, fear and disgust), while the left hemisphere processes the positive aspects of emotion that lead to approaching behaviors (for example, laughter and joy).

Moir and Jessel (1991) have suggested that the average male brain appears to follow this pattern of hemisphere specialization, while the average female brain may diffuse more emotional processing across the two hemispheres. If true, these organizational differences may help to explain commonly observed gender differences in emotional processing.

Time: The neocortex is divided into sensory and frontal lobes along an imaginary line drawn along our skull from ear to ear. Sensory lobes in the back store sensory memories (the past). Frontal lobes focus on critical thinking and problem-solving strategies (the present), with the front part of the lobes in charge of planning and rehearsal activities (the future).

The frontal lobes play an important role in regulating our emotional states and judgments. Our frontal lobe's regulation of critical thinking and problem solving permits it to override the execution of automatic behaviors, and of potentially destructive illegal or immoral behaviors that are sparked by emotional biases.

CLASSROOM APPLICATIONS

Although the educational applications of emotion research are still quite tentative, several general themes are emerging—and they tend to support a perspective that many educators have long advocated. This isn't surprising, since we're continually learning what does and doesn't work when dealing with students' emotions. What this research may provide, however, is biological support for the profession's beliefs.

Here are some general principles and their applications to the classroom:

1.   Emotions simply exist; we don't learn them in the same way we learn telephone numbers, and we can't easily change them. But we should not ignore them. Students can learn how and when to use rational processes to override their emotions, or to hold them in check. *We should seek to develop forms of self-control among students and staff that encourage nonjudgmental, nondisruptive (and perhaps even inefficient) venting of emotion* that generally must occur before reason can take over. We all can recall past incidents that still anger us because we were not allowed to freely express our feelings before a decision was imposed on us.

Integrating emotional expression in classroom life is not diffi-cult. Try drawing a class into a tension-releasing circle (after a play-ground fight, for example) and playing a game of circle tag before talking out the problem. Once the students' collective limbic systems have had their say, rational cortical processes can settle the issue. If that doesn't work, sing a song. (As British playwright William Congreve suggested, "Music hath charms to soothe a savage breast.") In other words, when trying to solve a problem, continue the dia-logue with continuous emotional input.

2.   Most students already know quite a bit about the complex-ity of emotions and the ways they and others experience them (Saarni and Harris 1991), although they may not be able to articulate what they know. *Schools should focus more on metacognitive activities that encourage students to talk about their emotions, listen to their classmates' feelings,* and think about the motivations of people who enter their curricular world. For example, the simple use of *why* in a question turns the discussion away from bare facts and toward moti-vations and emotions. *Why* did the pioneers settle where the two rivers came together? is a much more emotionally loaded question than *Where* did the pioneers settle?

3.   *Activities that emphasize social interaction and that engage the entire body tend to provide the most emotional support.* Games, discussions, field trips, interactive projects, cooperative learning,

physical education, and the arts are examples. Although we've long known that such activities enhance student learning, we tend to think of them as special rewards, and so withdraw them when students misbehave, or when budgets are tight, eliminate them altogether.

    4.   Memories are contextual. *School activities that draw out emotions—simulations, role playing, and cooperative projects, for example—may provide important contextual memory prompts* that will help students recall the information during closely related events in the real world. This is why we tend to practice fire drills in an unannounced, emotionally charged setting: in the event of a real fire, students will have to perform in that kind of setting.

    5.   *Emotionally stressful school environments are counterproductive because they can reduce students' ability to learn.* Self-esteem and a sense of control over one's environment are important in managing stress. Highly evaluative and authoritarian schools may promote institutional economy, efficiency, and accountability, but also heighten nonproductive stress in students and staff.

    In short, we need to think of students as more than mere brain tissue and bodies. Powerful peptides convert that body and brain tissue into a vibrant life force—the whole child that John Dewey urged us to educate.

REFERENCES

Corballis, M. (1991). *The Lopsided Ape: Evolution of the Generative Mind.* New York: Oxford University Press.

Edelman, G. (1992). *Bright Air, Brilliant Fire: On the Matter of the Mind.* New York: Basic.

Gazzaniga, M. (1989). *Mind Matters: How Mind and Brain Interact to Create Our Conscious Lives.* Boston: Houghton Mifflin.

Kandel, M. and E. Kandel. (May 1994). "Flights of Memory." *Discover Magazine,* 32–38.

Levinthal, C. (1988). *Messengers of Paradise: Opiates and the Brain.* New York: Doubleday.

Moir, A., and D. Jessel. (1991). *Brain Sex: The Real Difference Between Men and Women.* New York: Doubleday.

Moyers, B. (1992). *Healing and the Mind*. New York: Doubleday.

Saarni, C., and P. Harris, ed. (1991). *Children's Understanding of Emotion*. New York: Cambridge University Press.

Thayer, R. (1989). *The Biopsychology of Mood and Arousal*. New York: Oxford University Press.

Vincent, J-D. (1990). *The Biology of Emotions*. Cambridge, Mass.: Basil Blackwell.

The Neurobiology of Self-Esteem and Aggression

by Robert Sylwester

Self-esteem and serotonin—what can we learn from recent neurobiological research about how to help students work together cooperatively and successfully?

Violent acts like gang-related murders, playground shootings, riots, suicides, and assaults in school are prominently featured in the news, but they aren't the norm in social interactions. Young males commit most of the physically violent acts, and 7 percent of the population commits 80 percent of all the violent acts. Thus, violence is a limited social pathology, but one that evolutionary psychologists seek to explain because of its distressing, even tragic, results. Since impulsive behavior can lead to reckless or violently aggressive behavior, we also seek to understand impulsivity. Many personal and social problems begin with an impulsive act—triggered perhaps by the aggressor's low level of self-esteem. Impulsivity, recklessness, violence—all these behaviors can negatively affect educational processes. Some recent related research developments in brain chemistry—particularly the effects of the neurotransmitter serotonin—shed light on educational practices.

SELF-ESTEEM IN A HIERARCHY

Consider the following scenario—from the point of view of a neurobiologist studying social hierarchies or an evolutionary psychologist studying human behavior:

From *Educational Leadership,* February 1997, pp. 75–79. © 1997 by the Association for Supervision and Curriculum Development. All rights reserved. Reprinted with permission.

A young man joins an athletic team in his freshman year of high school. He's thrilled just to make the team, even though he knows he's low in the hierarchy and won't get to play much in games. He's content for now because he also knows that the coaches and his teammates will note every successful act he makes in scrimmage, and so his playing time will come. He moves up the team hierarchy, substituting a few minutes here and there. His competition for most of this journey isn't the *alpha males* at the top of the hierarchy, but, rather, those who are competing with him for the next slot in the hierarchy.

Over several years, his talent and that of his teammates will determine the level he achieves. He thus may settle for four years of comradeship, scrimmage, and limited game time because he realizes that's where he properly fits in the team hierarchy; or he may eventually bask in the celebrity afforded to him as one of the stars on the team. If the latter, he may seek to begin the sequence anew in a college team, and then perhaps a pro team. If the former, his memories and friendships will have to suffice—and he will seek success in other social arenas.

But what if he believes that he rates very high compared to the others—but the coaches don't agree, and won't give him a chance to play? Perhaps it's because of something he can't control, such as his height (or by extension, gender or race or whatever defines the *glass ceiling*). Imagine his frustration and rage. His opportunities don't match his sense of self.

It is adaptive for a social species (like humans) to develop a system that arranges groups into reasonably compatible hierarchical arrangements to perform various group tasks. The entire group benefits if survival-related tasks are assigned to those who are generally recognized to be the most capable. But things often don't work the way we'd like them to.

THE ROOTS OF VIOLENT AGGRESSION

The cognitive drive to move into our expected slot in the hierarchy is so strong that many people will do whatever it takes to achieve success. To continue with our sports scenario, if the frustration becomes too intense, a person may act impulsively or recklessly for any possible chance of success—and such risk-taking may on occasion escalate into aggressive and violent acts, which we may witness in news accounts of various sports, from baseball to Olympic-level figure skating.

Evolutionary psychology argues that each success enhances the level of the neurotransmitter *serotonin* in the brain—and so also our motor coordination and self-esteem (see box below). Failure and negative social feedback inhibit the effects of serotonin and lead to lower self-esteem and possible violence.

Serotonin and Prozac

Serotonin (hydroxytryptamine, or 5-HT) is a monamine neurotransmitter that enhances relaxation and smooth/controlled motor coordination (by inhibiting quick motor responses). It regulates intestinal peristalsis, cardiovascular function, endocrine secretion, mood, pain, sexual activity, appetite, and behavior and is probably (along with other neurotransmitters) involved in attention deficit disorders and seasonal affective disorder.

Serotonin is derived from the amino acid *tryptophan*. Wurtman found that carbohydrates in our diet enhance the entry of tryptophan into the brain, where it is converted into serotonin (Wurtman and Suffes 1996). Another neurotransmitter, *nitric oxide,* acts on serotonin to help curb aggressive behavior, as Nelson and colleagues (1995) found in studies with male mice.

Fluoxetine antidepressant drugs, such as Prozac, Zoloft, and Paxil, enhance the effects of serotonin. When neurotransmitters pass on their chemical message, most are then reabsorbed into the axon terminal and used again. These drugs block the *reuptake channels* on the terminal, and so slow down the reabsorption process (see fig. 1). This means that the serotonin neurotransmitters may activate receptors several times before being reabsorbed; thus, fluoxetine drugs increase the effectiveness of a limited discharge of serotonin without actually increasing the amount.

When young people see no hope to rise within mainstream society, they may create their own hierarchical gang cultures that provide them with opportunities to succeed within their counterculture's mores. Those among successful people in mainstream society who decry gang symbols and exclusionary turf areas should look to the high-status symbols they use to flaunt their success and to their exclusionary golf courses and walled communities. People in both mainstream cultures and countercultures have the same biological need to succeed; they all need a positive self-concept and self-esteem. Wealthy financiers have ruined small communities by closing moderately profitable plants for even greater profits elsewhere. Are such exploitative acts any less psychologically violent to the victims than the physical violence that erupts later in such communities from those whose plummeting serotonin levels suggest no vocational hope?

Recent research on stress (Sapolsky 1994) shows that in primate groups with a developed, stable hierarchy, those at the bottom (who had little control over events) experienced far more stress and stress-related illness than those at the top. Conversely, during periods in which the hierarchical structure was unstable and shifting, those currently at the top (whose power position was threatened) experienced the most stress and stress-related illness. This finding suggests that it is in the interest of the power elite (in community and classroom) to maintain social stability, and it is in the interest of the currently disenfranchised to create as much social instability (and classroom disruption) as possible in a desperate search for respect and success.

> The fewer opportunities young people have to succeed in mainstream society, the more social instability we can expect.

The fewer opportunities young people have to succeed in mainstream society, the more social instability we can expect. It is in our best interest to support inclusionary policies that promote social goals and to enhance the powerful role that schools can play in helping students to seek their dreams.

OUR BRAIN AND SOCIAL SYSTEMS

Our brain's complex collections of neural networks process our cognitive activity. Several dozen neurotransmitter and hormonal systems provide the key chemical substrate of this marvelous information-processing system. Neurotransmitter molecules, which are produced within one neuron, are released from that neuron's axon terminal into the synaptic gap, where they attach to receptors on the dendrites or surface of the next neuron in the information sequence (see fig. 1).

Recent studies with human and nonhuman primates suggest that fluctuations in the neurotransmitter serotonin play an important role in regulating our level of self-esteem and our place within the social hierarchy. Researchers associate high serotonin levels in the brain with high self-esteem and social status and low serotonin levels with low self-esteem and social status. High serotonin levels are associated with the calm assurance that leads to smoothly controlled movements, and low serotonin levels with the irritability that leads to impulsive, uncontrolled, reckless, aggressive, violent, or suicidal behavior.

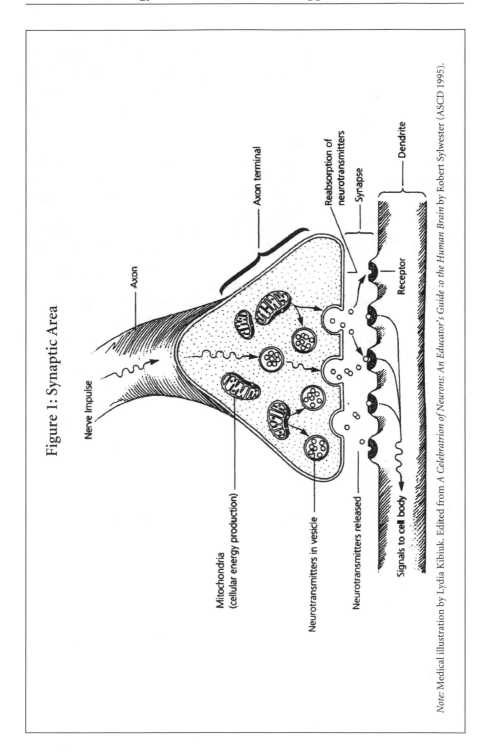

Figure 1: Synaptic Area

Note: Medical illustration by Lydia Kibiuk. Edited from *A Celebration of Neurons: An Educator's Guide to the Human Brain* by Robert Sylwester (ASCD 1995).

Evolutionary psychologists focus on the biological underpinnings of such educationally significant concepts as self-esteem, impulsivity, and aggression and on the effects of drugs like Prozac. If genetics and fluctuations in biochemical systems combine to trigger aggression, for example, one could argue that chronically aggressive people have a reduced capacity for free will and thus are not (legally) responsible for their acts. Further, if courts mandate medical treatments for such people, the policy could be viewed as governmental *mind control.* The social implications of this research are profound and wide ranging. For example, in determining responsibility for an aggressive act, how important are the negative effects of the aggressor's life experiences and the events that triggered the aggression?

> ... social feedback creates fluctuations from our basal serotonin levels, and these fluctuations help determine our current level of self-esteem.

Wright (1995) suggests that social feedback creates fluctuations from our basal serotonin levels, and these fluctuations help determine our current level of self-esteem. Thus, serotonin fluctuations are adaptive in that they help primates to negotiate social hierarchies, to move up as far as circumstances permit, and to be reasonably content at each stage, as our earlier sports scenario suggests. Social success elevates our self-esteem (and serotonin levels), and each such elevation further raises our social expectations, perhaps to try for a promotion or leadership role we hadn't considered when we were lower on the hierarchy.

A biological system of variability in self-esteem prepares and encourages us to reach and maintain a realistic level of social status. A high or low level of self-esteem (and serotonin) isn't innate and permanent. Successful people may tumble precipitously in social status, self-esteem, and serotonin levels when they retire or are discharged and thereby may experience a rapid reduction in positive social feedback. This doesn't mean that the serotonin system developed to help low-status people endure their fate for the good of all. Evolutionary psychology argues that natural selection rarely designs things for the good of the group. But the serotonin system provides us with a way to cope in a bad social situation—to be content to play a group role that is consistent with our current limitations. The human serotonin system seems to function similarly in males and females in the important roles it plays in regulating self-esteem and impulse control.

THE ROLE OF DRUGS AND NUTRITION

Is it possible to stimulate the serotonin system when conditions become so averse in a person's life that self-esteem and serotonin levels plummet into the depths of depression? Drugs such as Prozac (a fluoxetine antidepressant; see box on page 43) can produce an elevation in the effects of serotonin that often enhances a person's self-esteem; this increased optimism and happier mood leads to the positive social feedback that allows the natural system to take over again in time and to function effectively. Think of jump-starting a dead car battery—a few miles of driving will reenergize the battery, and it can then function on its own.

> The best support for a serotonin deficiency is probably the natural system of positive feedback that we have evolved over millennia.

People often use alcohol when they feel low, and alcohol does increase serotonin levels. Thus, it can temporarily help to raise our mood and self-esteem—but chronic alcohol use depletes a brain's store of serotonin, and so it makes matters even worse by further impairing the impulse control system.

Nutrition may provide another avenue to serotonin elevation. Prolonged periods of stress increase our brain's need for serotonin. Nutrition researchers have discovered a connection between serotonin/carbohydrate levels and emotionally driven eating disorders that emerge out of family stress, premenstrual syndrome, shift work, seasonal mood changes, and the decision to stop smoking. Wurtman and Suffes (1996) propose nondrug diet adaptations that could solve some of these problems.

Prescription and other drugs can provide only a temporary chemical boost in self-esteem, and diets require a certain level of self-control. The best support for a serotonin deficiency is probably the natural system of positive social feedback that we have evolved over millennia.

EDUCATIONAL IMPLICATIONS

If positive social feedback is nature's way of regulating the serotonin system so that both an inexperienced substitute football player and the team's star can work together comfortably and effectively, then positive feedback in the classroom is a powerful social device for helping us to assess and define ourselves (self-concept) and to value ourselves (self-esteem). Serotonin research adds biological support to some educational practices that enhance self-esteem—and these practices don't require a prescription or an ID card that proves you are 21 years old.

• Portfolio assessments encourage self-examination in students and enhance student self-concept and self-esteem. Journals, creative artwork, and other forms of reflective thought can produce the same results.

• When students have many opportunities to work together in groups, they may experience success in both leading and supporting roles. Positive self-esteem can develop at any level in a work group, if the problem is challenging and the group values the contributions of all.

• Many school conflicts arise because an impulsive, reckless act escalates into aggression. We have tended to view these events only in negative terms—as misbehavior, as something to be squashed. But what if we used positive group strategies to help students study such behavior and discover how to reduce it? David and Roger Johnson (1995) provide practical cooperative learning strategies for conflict resolution that are consistent with neurobiological research.

• Emmy Werner's four-decade longitudinal study of seriously at-risk children who matured into resilient, successful adults found that they received unconditional love from family or nonfamily mentors, who encouraged their curiosity, interests, and dreams and assigned them responsibilities that helped them to discover their strengths and weaknesses (Werner and Smith 1992). We can also provide this support in the classroom—and parents, guardians, and other community members can help.

Cognitive science research is now providing some welcome biological support for practices that many educators have felt were *simply right,* even though these strategies take more instructional time and energy and result in less precise evaluations. Serotonin was identified as a neurotransmitter at about the time that Werner began her studies of resilient at-risk children in 1955—with no hint of the powerful biological substrate of her research. That kind of research is now becoming available to us. Let's use it.

USEFUL RESOURCES

Bower, B. (April 15, 1995). "Criminal Intellects: Researchers Look at Why Law-breakers Often Brandish Low I.Q.'s." *Science News* 147, 15: 232–239.

Coccaro, E. (January/February 1995). "Biology of Aggression." *Scientific American Science and Medicine:* 38–47.

Fuller, R. (July/August 1995). "Neural Functions of Serotonin." *Scientific American Science and Medicine* 2, 4: 48–57.

Goleman, D. (1995). *Emotional Intelligence: Why It Can Matter More Than I.Q.* New York: Bantam.

Hobson, J. (1994). *The Chemistry of Conscious States: How the Brain Changes Its Mind.* Boston: Little, Brown.

Johnson, D., and R. Johnson. (1995). *Reducing School Violence Through Conflict Resolution.* Alexandria, Va.: ASCD.

Kramer, P. (1994). *Listening to Prozac.* New York: Penguin.

Masters, R., and M. McGuire, eds. (1994). *The Neurotransmitter Revolution: Serotonin, Social Behavior, and the Law.* Carbondale, Ill.: Southern Illinois University Press.

Nelson, R., S. Snyder, and Others. (November 23, 1995). "Behavioral Abnormalities in Male Mice Lacking Neuronal Nitric Oxide Synthase." *Nature* 378: 383–388.

Nesse, R., and G. Williams. (1994). *Why We Get Sick: The New Science of Darwinian Medicine.* New York: Random House.

Restak, R. (1994). *Receptors.* New York: Bantam.

Sapolsky, R. (1994). *Why Zebras Don't Get Ulcers: A Guide to Stress, Stress-Related Diseases, and Coping.* New York: Freeman.

Volavka, J. (1995). *The Neurobiology of Violence.* Washington, D.C.: American Psychiatric Press.

Werner, E., and R. Smith. (1992). *Overcoming the Odds: High Risk Children from Birth to Adulthood.* Ithaca, N.Y.: Cornell University Press.

Wright, R. (1994). *The Moral Animal, Why We Are the Way We Are: The New Science of Evolutionary Psychology.* New York: Pantheon.

Wright, R. (March 13, 1995). "The Biology of Violence." *The New Yorker:* 68–77.

Wurtman, J., and S. Suffes. (1996). *The Serotonin Solution: The Potent Brain Chemical That Can Help You Stop Bingeing, Lose Weight, and Feel Great.* New York: Fawcett Columbine.

Can't Do Without Love

What science says about those tender feelings

by Shannon Brownlee

Love has toppled kings, inspired poets, sparked wars, soothed beasts, and changed the course of history. It is credited for life's greatest joys, blamed for the most crushing sorrows. And of course, it "makes the world go round."

All of which is no surprise to biologists. They know that love is central to human existence. We are not just programmed for reproduction: The capacity for loving emotions is also written into our biochemistry, essential if children are to grow and to thrive. And love's absence can be devastating: The loss of a spouse often hastens death in older people.

Now researchers are beginning to sort out how body and mind work together to produce the wild, tender, ineffable feelings we call love. They have found, for example, that oxytocin, a chemical that fosters the bond between mothers and children, probably helps fuel romantic love as well. Brain chemicals that blunt pain and induce feelings of euphoria may also make people feel good in the company of lovers. And certain other mammals share many of the same neural and chemical pathways involved in human love—though no one knows if they feel a similar swooning intensity of emotion.

Far from reducing love's thrill to dry facts, biologists' efforts underscore the emotion's importance. "We evolved as social organisms," says University of Maryland zoologist Sue Carter. "The study of love tells us that we have a biology that allows us to be good to each other."

From *U.S. News & World Report,* February 17, 1997, pp. 58–60. © 1997, U.S. News & World Report. Reprinted with permission.

MOTHER, MOTHER

Love began with motherhood. For mammalian young to survive, mothers must invest considerable time and energy in them. Of course, the varying growth rates of mammalian species require some mothers to invest more time and energy than others. An elephant seal suckles her pup for only a few weeks before abandoning it; other species, including elephants, some primates, and especially people, lavish attention on their young for years.

With the help of oxytocin, doting mothers are able to cater to their offspring's every whim and whimper. When females of most mammalian species give birth, their bodies are flooded with oxytocin, known since 1906 as a hormone that stimulates uterine contractions and allows the breasts to "let down" milk. But oxytocin also acts as a neurotransmitter, or chemical messenger, that can guide behavior. Without it, a ewe cannot recognize her own lamb. A virgin female rat given a shot of oxytocin will nuzzle another female's pups, crouching over them protectively as if they were her own.

> Mothers with higher levels of oxytocin are more sensitive to other people's feelings and better at reading nonverbal cues . . .

Oxytocin has even more dramatic effects on human mothers, inducing a tender openness that fosters maternal devotion. As a mother breast-feeds, oxytocin levels rise in her blood. She also scores higher on psychological measures of "social desirability," the urge to please others, according to Kerstin Uvnas-Moberg of Sweden's Karolinska Institute. Mothers with higher levels of oxytocin are more sensitive to other people's feelings and better at reading nonverbal cues than those with lower levels. This makes sense, says Uvnas-Moberg, because oxytocin is thought to bind to centers in the brain involved with emotion. In her most recent experiments, the scientist has found that oxytocin acts as a natural tranquilizer, lowering a new mother's blood pressure, blunting her sensitivity to pain and stress, and perhaps helping her view her child more as a bundle of joy than as a burden.

Studies of a small rodent known as the prairie vole, a cuddly ball of fur whose mating bond of lifelong monogamy would put most human couples to shame, indicate oxytocin may also play a role in the heady feelings associated with romance. "You just can't imagine how much time these animals spend together. Prairie voles always want to be with somebody," says Carter. The voles' undying devotion is the work not only of oxytocin but also of a related hormone, vasopressin. When single male and female prairie voles meet, they commence a two-day-long bout of sex that releases oxytocin in the female's brain, bonding her to the male. Deprived of the chemical, she finds him no more appealing than any other vole. Given an injection of oxytocin, she will prefer the vole she's with, whether or not they have consummated their relationship. Vasopressin inspires similar ardor in the male, who prefers his mate's company above all others, guarding his family against intruders with a jealous husband's zeal.

> **Human beings—unlike rodents—are not entirely slaves to their hormones.**

Like some human playboys, male prairie voles seem to get a kick out of courtship mixed with danger. Carter and colleague Courtney DeVries made young, unmated voles swim for three minutes before allowing them to meet a prospective mate. The exercise elevated the animals' stress hormones, which are also heightened by fear. But while females scurried off after the swim without bonding to the males as they normally would, male voles bonded faster than ever.

LURE OF THE FORBIDDEN

Human beings—unlike rodents—are not entirely slaves to their hormones. But the behavior of voles may hold clues to why men and women sometimes hold divergent views of sex and romance. While many women prefer candlelight and sweet talk, men are more apt to welcome a roll in the hay anytime, anywhere. For some men (and some women), sex is especially enticing when forbidden. Carter and DeVries suspect stress hormones can interfere with oxytocin's action in the brain, keeping a female vole from bonding, and perhaps preventing most women from finding danger sexually exciting. Vasopressin, in contrast, appears to work better in the presence of certain stress hormones, possibly making danger an aphrodisiac for many males.

Love's other messengers in the brain are the endorphins, or brain opiates—the body's own version of drugs such as heroin and morphine. High levels of brain opiates kill pain and induce a state of happy relaxation. Low levels are associated with unpleasant feelings. Researchers believe the power of endorphins to affect mood may play a crucial role in bonding.

Compelling evidence for this notion comes from recent studies of female talapoin monkeys, animals that form what in humans would be termed friendships. While male talapoins are bellicose and standoffish, female talapoin friends spend as much as a third of their day grooming each other and twining their long tails together. Barry Keverne, a primatologist at Cambridge University in England, has found that when talapoin friends who have been separated are reunited, they commence grooming enthusiastically—and their endorphins skyrocket to double the usual level. Separated monkeys given a low dose of morphine, however, show little interest in grooming upon reunion: Since their opiate levels are already high, they don't need each other to feel good again. "It's not surprising that the same opioid system that evolved to modulate physical pain also can soothe the pain of social isolation," says Jaak Panksepp of Ohio's Bowling Green State University.

> ... it's not unlikely that human lovers and friends enjoy a soothing surge of endorphins when they meet—and miss that feeling when separated.

Indeed, research on opiates suggests the flip side of love is not hate, but grief. "Biochemically, loss of love, or grief, is the inverse of love," says Keverne. Nobody has yet proved that people get an endorphin kick out of love or friendship. But the human brain shares so much of its emotional chemistry with close evolutionary relatives, it's not unlikely that human lovers and friends enjoy a soothing surge of endorphins when they meet—and miss that feeling when separated.

Passionate or platonic, love affects the whole body, setting the heart pounding, making the stomach do flip-flops, and of course, lighting the loins on fire. These visceral sensations are the work of the vagus nerve, which traces a meandering path through the body, coordinating the activities of internal organs, says the University of Maryland's Stephen Porges. The vagus ferries signals between our innards and our brains, conveying information upward about our internal state and sending orders down from the brain to the heart, the stomach, the lungs, and the sex organs.

Without the vagus, says Porges, love would be impossible. One part of the nerve is evolutionarily ancient, controlling primitive functions such as sex, hunger, and fear. This "old" vagus responds to oxytocin and serves as the pathway between sexual organs and the brain for feelings of both arousal and satiation after sex. But Porges argues that in mammals, newer branches of the vagus also connect emotional brain centers with the heart, the face, and the vocal equipment, helping to coordinate feelings with facial and verbal expression. The "new" vagus also helps slow the heart and keep the body calm enough for the brain to pay attention to emotional signals from other people. Without this, says Porges, "we can't modulate our interiors enough to express or read emotions."

In other words, the poets and bards were right about one thing: The heart speaks the language of love. As English poet W. II. Auden wrote, *Where love is strengthened, hope restored, /In hearts by chemical accord.* It may not literally skip a beat at the sight of one's desire or break with sorrow, but the heart's rhythms are exquisitely tuned to love.

RECOMMENDED READINGS

Brothers, Leslie. *Friday's Footprints: How Society Shapes the Human Mind.* New York: Oxford Press, 1997.
An excellent nontechnical exploration of the neurobiology of social behavior by a noted authority on autism (the converse of social behavior). Brothers argues persuasively for procedures that enhance social development.

Damasio, Antonio. *Descartes' Error: Emotion, Reason, and the Human Brain.* New York: Grossett/Putnam, 1994.
An eloquent, thoughtful, nontechnical discussion of the nature of emotion by a principal researcher in the field of emotion. He explains the importance of emotion to rational behavior.

Goleman, Daniel. *Emotional Intelligence: Why It Can Matter More Than IQ.* New York: Bantam, 1995.
The book that introduced many educators and others to the dramatic advances in emotion research. An excellent, easily understood, nontechnical synthesis of the research.

LeDoux, Joseph. *The Emotional Brain: The Mysterious Underpinnings of Emotional Life.* New York: Simon and Schuster, 1996.
LeDoux is a major researcher on the emotion of fear, certainly a key emotion. Fear is educationally significant since many students regrettably live in fearful home and/or school environments. This is an excellent explanation of the neurobiology of fear, with useful suggestions for regulating it.

Pert, Candace. *The Molecules of Emotion: Why You Feel the Way You Feel.* New York: Scribners, 1997.
Pert made major discoveries about the endorphins, key molecules in the regulation of pain and euphoria. This simply delightful let-it-all-hang-out book is part autobiography and part thoughtful explanation of the author's somewhat controversial views on emotion. Many educators would agree with her expansive views of what constitutes emotion.

Ridley, Matt. *The Origins of Virtue: Human Instincts and the Evolution of Cooperation.* New York: Norton, 1996.
A thoughtful, fascinating discussion of the innate and social forces that enhance cooperation and collaboration among humans—when conventional wisdom believes we're basically competitive and operate mostly out of self-interest.

Salovey, Peter, and David Sluyter, editors. *Emotional Development and Emotional Intelligence: Educational Implications.* New York: Basic Books, 1997.

Elias, Maurice, and others. *Promoting Social and Emotional Learning: Guidelines for Educators.* Alexandria, VA: Association for Supervision and Curriculum Development, 1997.

Two fine books that apply recent emotion research to classroom life. Peter Salovey is the person who first proposed the concept of emotional intelligence that Daniel Goleman expanded into the book, *Emotional Intelligence.* Both books are a wealth of useful information for educators.

Biological and Techno-logical Perspectives on Intelligence

cientists have discovered that humans have a modular brain. Discrete areas are specialized for processing highly specific tasks (such as line segments, colors, and textures), and many widely distributed brain areas collaborate in processing a complex task (such as to recognize a friend). This has led to the current belief that a single one-size-fits-all measure of intelligence, such as the IQ, is inadequate to explain the complexities of intelligent behavior.

Our brains must adapt themselves to a world in which our personal and social identities interact effectively with natural space and/or time. Therefore, a major intellectual challenge is to effectively understand and use personal/social identities, space/place, and time/sequence in our daily lives. Howard Gardner is a major theorist in the field of intelligence whose eight (and possibly nine) forms of intelligence fit nicely into this biological framework:

• Personal/Social Identities: intrapersonal, interpersonal, and existential intelligences
• Space/Place: visual/spatial, bodily/kinesthetic, and naturalist intelligences
• Time/Sequence: verbal/linguistic, musical/rhythmic, and logical/mathematical intelligences

Robert Sternberg is another major intelligence theorist. His triarchic mind model also focuses on three major intellectual concerns, which he defines as creative, analytic, and practical intelligences. These forms of intelligence are more process oriented—how one acts intelligently—rather than the identification of mental areas in which an intelligent brain functions. Thus, one could think of Gardner's forms of intelligence as nouns and Sternberg's as verbs. Perhaps intelligence is the marvelous blend that we call a sentence.

In the first two articles in this section, Gardner and Sternberg discuss the current state of their theories and the evidence of their effectiveness. The recommended readings list their two most recent books. Both are excellent and are strongly recommended for anyone interested in issues that surround the nature and measurement of intelligence.

We have had eons to tune into natural space and time but only a few years to try to understand electronic space and time (or cyberspace and cybertime). The electronic world can do things the natural world couldn't hope to do—speed up the flowering of a rose via time-lapse photography, enlarge a microscopic organism, send information via a satellite all over the world, and rapidly connect geographically dispersed groups of people via e-mail.

When I was a child, my parents taught me the joys and dangers of parks (such as that swings can be both fun and dangerous), but they eventually had to let me explore the parks on my own. Today's parents now must also deal with an electronic park called the Internet that also has its joys and dangers. A 12-year-old boy on a chat line pretending to be a 20-year-old woman can chat with a 35-year-old woman pretending to be a 20-year-old man. Talk about an identity crisis! One problem is that most parents (and educators) have an innate understanding of natural space and time but they lag well behind their children in understanding the cyberspace and cybertime of our electronic world and thus are hampered in their ability to help young people to properly explore that world.

The final two articles in this section explore neurobiological, parental, and educational issues that surround the intelligent use of the electronic revolution that's currently drag racing the cognitive science revolution into the twenty-first century. Moursund's article on forecasts for technology in education is an especially authoritative analysis of that important issue. It's an excerpt from his highly recommended book, *The Future of Information Technology in Education*, listed in the recommended readings.

The First Seven . . . and the Eighth: A Conversation with Howard Gardner

by Kathy Checkley

Howard Gardner's theory of multiple intelligences, described in *Frames of Mind* (1985), sparked a revolution of sorts in classrooms around the world, a mutiny against the notion that human beings have a single, fixed intelligence. The fervor with which educators embraced his premise that we have multiple intelligences surprised Gardner himself. "It obviously spoke to some sense that people had that kids weren't all the same and that the tests we had only skimmed the surface about the differences among kids," Gardner said.

Here Gardner brings us up-to-date on his current thinking on intelligence, how children learn, and how they should be taught.

H*ow do you define intelligence?*
Intelligence refers to the human ability to solve problems or to make something that is valued in one or more cultures. As long as we can find a culture that values an ability to solve a problem or create a product in a particular way, then I would strongly consider whether that ability should be considered an intelligence.

First, though, that ability must meet other criteria: Is there a particular representation in the brain for the ability? Are there populations that are especially good or especially impaired in an intelligence? And, can an evolutionary history of the intelligence be seen in animals other than human beings?

I defined seven intelligences (see box, page 63) in the early 1980s because those intelligences all fit the criteria. A decade later when I revisited the task, I found at least one more ability that clearly deserved to be called an intelligence.

That would be the naturalist intelligence. What led you to consider adding this to our collection of intelligences?

Somebody asked me to explain the achievements of the great biologists, the ones who had a real mastery of taxonomy, who understood about different species, who could recognize patterns in nature and classify objects. I realized that to explain that kind of ability, I would have to manipulate the other intelligences in ways that weren't appropriate.

So I began to think about whether the capacity to classify nature might be a separate intelligence. The naturalist ability passed with flying colors. Here are a couple of reasons: First, it's an ability we need to survive as human beings. We need, for example, to know which animals to hunt and which to run away from. Second, this ability isn't restricted to human beings. Other animals need to have a naturalist intelligence to survive. Finally, the big selling point is that brain evidence supports the existence of the naturalist intelligence. There are certain parts of the brain particularly dedicated to the recognition and the naming of what are called "natural" things.

How do you describe the naturalist intelligence to those of us who aren't psychologists?

The naturalist intelligence refers to the ability to recognize and classify plants, minerals, and animals, including rocks and grass and all variety of flora and fauna. The ability to recognize cultural artifacts like cars or sneakers may also depend on the naturalist intelligence.

Now, everybody can do this to a certain extent—we can all recognize dogs, cats, trees. But, some people from an early age are extremely good at recognizing and classifying artifacts. For example, we all know kids who, at age 3 or 4, are better at recognizing dinosaurs than most adults.

Darwin is probably the most famous example of a naturalist because he saw so deeply into the nature of living things.

The Intelligences, in Gardner's Words

- Linguistic intelligence is the capacity to use language, your native language, and perhaps other languages, to express what's on your mind and to understand other people. Poets really specialize in linguistic intelligence, but any kind of writer, orator, speaker, lawyer, or a person for whom language is an important stock in trade highlights linguistic intelligence.
- People with a highly developed logical-mathematical intelligence understand the underlying principles of some kind of a causal system, the way a scientist or a logician does; or can manipulate numbers, quantities, and operations, the way a mathematician does.
- Spatial intelligence refers to the ability to represent the spatial world internally in your mind—the way a sailor or airplane pilot navigates the large spatial world, or the way a chess player or sculptor represents a more circumscribed spatial world. Spatial intelligence can be used in the arts or in the sciences. If you are spatially intelligent and oriented toward the arts, you are more likely to become a painter or a sculptor or an architect than, say, a musician or a writer. Similarly, certain sciences like anatomy or topology emphasize spatial intelligence.
- Bodily kinesthetic intelligence is the capacity to use your whole body or parts of your body—your hand, your fingers, your arms—to solve a problem, make something, or put on some kind of a production. The most evident examples are people in athletics or the performing arts, particularly dance or acting.
- Musical intelligence is the capacity to think in music, to be able to hear patterns, recognize them, remember them, and perhaps manipulate them. People who have a strong musical intelligence don't just remember music easily—they can't get it out of their minds, it's so omnipresent. Now, some people will say, "Yes, music is important, but it's a talent, not an intelligence." And I say, "Fine, let's call it a talent." But, then we have to leave the word *intelligent* out of *all* discussions of human abilities. You know, Mozart was damned smart!
- Interpersonal intelligence is understanding other people. It's an ability we all need, but is at a premium if you are a teacher, clinician, salesperson, or politician. Anybody who deals with other people has to be skilled in the interpersonal sphere.
- Intrapersonal intelligence refers to having an understanding of yourself, of knowing who you are, what you can do, what you want to do, how you react to things, which things to avoid, and which things to gravitate toward. We are drawn to people who have a good understanding of themselves because those people tend not to screw up. They tend to know what they can do. They tend to know what they can't do. And they tend to know where to go if they need help.
- Naturalist intelligence designates the human ability to discriminate among living things (plants, animals) as well as sensitivity to other features of the natural world (clouds, rock configurations). This ability was clearly of value in our evolutionary past as hunters, gatherers, and farmers; it continues to be central in such roles as botanist or chef. I also speculate that much of our consumer society exploits the naturalist intelligences, which can be mobilized in the discrimination among cars, sneakers, kinds of makeup, and the like. The kind of pattern recognition valued in certain of the sciences may also draw upon naturalist intelligence.

Are there any other abilities you're considering calling intelligences?

Well, there may be an existential intelligence that refers to the human inclination to ask very basic questions about existence. Who are we? Where do we come from? What's it all about? Why do we die? We might say that existential intelligence allows us to know the invisible, outside world. The only reason I haven't given a seal of approval to the existential intelligence is that I don't think we have good brain evidence yet on its existence in the nervous system—one of the criteria for an intelligence.

> If we treat everybody as if they were the same, we're catering to one profile of intelligence, the language-logic profile.

You have said that the theory of multiple intelligences may be best understood when we know what it critiques. What do you mean?

The standard view of intelligence is that intelligence is something you are born with; you have only a certain amount of it; you cannot do much about how much of that intelligence you have; and tests exist that can tell you how smart you are. The theory of multiple intelligences challenges that view. It asks, instead, "Given what we know about the brain, evolution, and the differences in cultures, what are the sets of human abilities we all share?"

My analysis suggested that rather than one or two intelligences, all human beings have several (eight) intelligences. What makes life interesting, however, is that we don't have the same strength in each intelligence area, and we don't have the same amalgam of intelligences. Just as we look different from one another and have different kinds of personalities, we also have different kinds of minds.

This premise has very serious educational implications. If we treat everybody as if they are the same, we're catering to one profile of intelligence, the language-logic profile. It's great if you have that profile, but it's not great for the vast majority of human beings who do not have that particular profile of intelligence.

Can you explain more fully how the theory of multiple intelligences challenges what has become known as IQ?

The theory challenges the entire notion of IQ. The IQ test was developed about a century ago as a way to determine who would have trouble in school. The test measures linguistic ability, logical-mathematical ability, and, occasionally, spatial ability.

What the intelligence test does not do is inform us about our other intelligences; it also doesn't look at other virtues like creativity or civic mindedness, or whether a person is moral or ethical.

We don't do much IQ testing anymore, but the shadow of IQ tests is still with us because the SAT—arguably the most potent examination in the world—is basically the same kind of disembodied language-logic instrument.

The truth is, I don't believe there is such a general thing as scholastic aptitude. Even so, I don't think that the SAT will fade until colleges indicate that they'd rather have students who know how to use their minds well—students who may or may not be good test takers, but who are serious, inquisitive, and know how to probe and problem-solve. That is really what college professors want, I believe.

> . . . any topic of importance, from any discipline, can be taught in more than one way.

Can we strengthen our intelligences? If so, how?

We can all get better at each of the intelligences, although some people will improve in an intelligence area more readily than others, either because biology gave them a better brain for that intelligence or because their culture gave them a better teacher.

Teachers have to help students use their combination of intelligences to be successful in school, to help them learn whatever it is they want to learn, as well as what the teachers and society believe they have to learn.

Now, I'm not arguing that kids shouldn't learn the literacies. Of course they should learn the literacies. Nor am I arguing that kids shouldn't learn the disciplines. I'm a tremendous champion of the disciplines. What I argue against is the notion that there's only one way to learn how to read, only one way to learn how to compute, only one way to learn about biology. I think that such contentions are nonsense.

It's equally nonsensical to say that everything should be taught seven or eight ways. That's not the point of the MI theory. The point is to realize that any topic of importance, from any discipline, can be taught in more than one way. There are things people need to know, and educators have to be extraordinarily imaginative and persistent in helping students understand things better.

A popular activity among those who are first exploring multiple intelligences is to construct their own intellectual profile. It's thought that when teachers go through the process of creating such a profile, they're more likely to recognize and appreciate the intellectual strengths of their students. What is your view on this kind of activity?

My own studies have shown that people love to do this. Kids like to do it, adults like to do it. And, as an activity, I think it's perfectly harmless.

I get concerned, though, when people think that determining your intellectual profile—or that of someone else—is an end in itself.

You have to use the profile to understand the ways in which you seem to learn easily. And, from there, determine how to use those strengths to help you become more successful in other endeavors. Then, the profile becomes a way for you to understand yourself better, and you can use that understanding to catapult yourself to a better level of understanding or to a higher level of skill.

How has your understanding of the multiple intelligences influenced how you teach?

My own teaching has changed slowly as a result of multiple intelligences because I'm teaching graduate students psychological theory and there are only so many ways I can do that. I am more open to group work and to student projects of various sorts, but even if I wanted to be an "MI professor" of graduate students, I still have a certain moral obligation to prepare them for a world in which they will have to write scholarly articles and prepare theses.

Where I've changed much more, I believe, is at the workplace. I direct research projects and work with all kinds of people. Probably 10 to 15 years ago, I would have tried to find people who were just like me to work with me on these projects.

I've really changed my attitude a lot on that score. Now I think much more in terms of what people are good at and in putting together teams of people whose varying strengths complement one another.

How should thoughtful educators implement the theory of multiple intelligences?

Although there is no single MI route, it's very important that a teacher take individual differences among kids very seriously. You cannot be a good MI teacher if you don't want to know each child and try to gear how you teach and how you evaluate to that particular child. The bottom line is a deep interest in children and how their minds are different from one another, and in helping them use their minds well.

Now, kids can be great informants for teachers. For example, a teacher might say, "Look, Benjamin, this obviously isn't working. Should we try using a picture?" If Benjamin gets excited about that approach, that's a pretty good clue to the teacher about what could work.

The theory of multiple intelligences, in and of itself, is not going to solve anything in our society, but linking the multiple intelligences with a curriculum focused on understanding is an extremely powerful intellectual undertaking.

> **We know people truly understand something when they can represent the knowledge in more than one way.**

When I talk about understanding, I mean that students can take ideas they learn in school, or anywhere for that matter, and apply those appropriately in new situations. We know people truly understand something when they can represent the knowledge in more than one way. We have to put understanding up front in school. Once we have that goal, multiple intelligences can be a terrific handmaiden because understandings involve a mix of mental representations, entailing different intelligences.

People often say that what they remember most about school are those learning experiences that were linked to real life. How does the theory of multiple intelligences help connect learning to the world outside the classroom?

The theory of multiple intelligences wasn't based on school work or on tests. Instead, what I did was look at the world and ask, What are the things that people do in the world? What does it mean to be a surgeon? What does it mean to be a politician? What does it mean to be an artist or a sculptor? What abilities do you need to do those things? My theory, then, came from the things that are valued in the world.

So when a school values multiple intelligences, the relationship to what's valued in the world is patent. If you cannot easily relate this activity to something that's valued in the world, the school has probably lost the core idea of multiple intelligences, which is that these intelligences evolved to help people do things that matter in the real world.

School matters, but only insofar as it yields something that can be used once students leave school.

How can teachers be guided by multiple intelligences when creating assessment tools?

We need to develop assessments that are much more representative of what human beings are going to have to do to survive in this society. For example, I value literacy, but my measure of literacy should not be whether you can answer a multiple-choice question that asks you to select the best meaning of a paragraph. Instead, I'd rather have you read the paragraph and list four questions you have about the paragraph and figure out how you would answer those questions. Or, if I want to know how you can write, let me give you a stem and see whether you can write about that topic, or let me ask you to write an editorial in response to something you read in the newspaper or observed on the street.

> ... you could not really be an advocate of multiple intelligences if you didn't have some dissatisfaction with the current testing ...

The current emphasis on performance assessment is well supported by the theory of multiple intelligences. Indeed, you could not really be an advocate of multiple intelligences if you didn't have some dissatisfaction with the current testing because it's so focused on short-answer, linguistic, or logical kinds of items.

MI theory is very congenial to an approach that says: one, let's not look at things through the filter of a short-answer test. Let's look directly at the performance that we value, whether it's a linguistic, logical, aesthetic, or social performance; and, two, let's never pin our assessment of understanding on just one particular measure, but let's always allow students to show their understanding in a variety of ways.

You have identified several myths about the theory of multiple intelligences. Can you describe some of those myths?

One myth that I personally find irritating is that an intelligence is the same as a learning style. Learning styles are claims about ways in which individuals purportedly approach everything they do. If you are planful, you are supposed to be planful about everything. If you are logical-sequential, you are supposed to be logical-sequential about everything. My own research and observations suggest that that's a dubious assumption. But whether or not that's true, learning styles are very different from multiple intelligences.

> One myth that I personally find irritating is that an intelligence is the same as a learning style.

Multiple intelligences claims that we respond, individually, in different ways to different kinds of content, such as language or music or other people. This is very different from the notion of learning style.

You can say that a child is a visual learner, but that's not a multiple intelligences way of talking about things. What I would say is, "Here is a child who very easily represents things spatially, and we can draw upon that strength if need be when we want to teach the child something new."

Another widely believed myth is that, because we have seven or eight intelligences, we should create seven or eight tests to measure students' strengths in each of those areas. That is a perversion of the theory. It's re-creating the sin of the single intelligence quotient and just multiplying it by a larger number. I'm personally against assessment of intelligences unless such a measurement is used for a very specific learning purpose—we want to help a child understand her history or his mathematics better and, therefore, want to see what might be good entry points for that particular child.

What experiences led you to the study of human intelligence?

It's hard for me to pick out a single moment, but I can see a couple of snapshots. When I was in high school, my uncle gave me a textbook in psychology. I'd never actually heard of psychology before. This textbook helped me understand color blindness. I'm color blind, and I became fascinated by the existence of plates that illustrated what color blindness was. I could actually explain why I couldn't see colors.

Another time when I was studying the Reformation, I read a book by Erik Erikson called *Young Man Luther* (1958).[1] I was fascinated by the psychological motivation of Luther to attack the Catholic Church. That fascination influenced my decision to go into psychology.

The most important influence was actually learning about brain damage and what could happen to people when they had strokes. When a person has a stroke, a certain part of the brain gets injured, and that injury can tell you what that part of the brain does. Individuals who lose their musical abilities can still talk. People who lose their linguistic ability still might be able to sing. That understanding not only brought me into the whole world of brain study, but it was really the seed that led ultimately to the theory of multiple intelligences. As long as you can lose one ability while others are spared, you cannot just have a single intelligence. You have to have several intelligences.

NOTES

1. See Erik Erikson, *Young Man Luther* (New York: W. W. Norton, 1958).

What Does It Mean to Be Smart?

by Robert J. Sternberg

A Yale study, based on the premise that intelligence has analytical, creative, and practical aspects, shows that if schools start valuing all three, they may find that thousands of kids are smarter than they think.

The most widely circulated newspaper in Connecticut recently carried a story on the meteoric rise of the president of one of the major banks in the state. I might have passed over the story with a glance had the name of the bank president not caught my eye. He was someone with whom I had gone to school from 1st grade right up through high school. What especially caught my attention, though, was that he had been a *C* student—someone who didn't seem to have much to offer.

Were the bank president an isolated case it might not be cause for alarm. But one cannot help wondering how many such students conclude that they really do not have much to contribute—in school or in the world at large—and so never try.

THE COST OF A CLOSED SYSTEM

Our system of education is, to a large degree, a closed system. Students are tested and classified in terms of two kinds of abilities—their ability to memorize information and, to a lesser extent, their ability to analyze it. They are also taught and assessed in ways that emphasize memory and analysis. As a result, we label students who excel in these patterns of ability as smart or able. We may label students who are weaker in these abilities as average or even slow or stupid.

From *Educational Leadership,* March 1997, pp. 20–24. © 1997 by the Association for Supervision and Curriculum Development. All rights reserved. Reprinted with permission.

Students may, however, excel in other abilities that are at least as important as those we now reward. Creativity and the practical application of information—ordinary common sense or "street smarts"—are two such abilities that go unappreciated and unrecognized. They are simply not considered relevant to conventional education.

The ability tests we currently use, whether to measure intelligence or achievement or to determine college admissions, also value memory and analytical abilities. These tests predict school performance reasonably well. They do so because they emphasize the same abilities that are emphasized in the classroom.

> **Through grades and test scores, we may be rewarding only a fraction of the students who should be rewarded.**

Thus, students who excel in memory and analytical abilities get good grades. Practically oriented learners, however, who are better able to learn a set of facts if they can see its relevance to their own lives, lose out. (Indeed, many teachers and administrators are themselves practical learners who simply tune out lectures or workshops they consider irrelevant to them.)

The consequences of this system are potentially devastating. Through grades and test scores, we may be rewarding only a fraction of the students who should be rewarded. Worse, we may be inadvertently disenfranchising multitudes of students from learning. In fact, when researchers have examined the lives of enormously influential people, whether in creative domains (Gardner 1993), practical domains (Gardner 1995), or both, they have found that many of these people had been ordinary—or even mediocre—students.

TEACHING IN ALL FOUR WAYS

At any grade level and in any subject, we can teach and assess in a way that enables students to use all four abilities (Sternberg 1994, Sternberg and Spear-Swerling 1996. See also Sternberg and Williams 1996, Williams et al. 1996). In other words, we can ask students to

- Recall who did something, what was done, when it was done, where it was done, or how it was done;
- Analyze, compare, evaluate, judge, or assess;
- Create, invent, imagine, suppose, or design; and
- Use, put into practice, implement, or show use.

In physical education, for example, competitors need to learn and remember various strategies for playing games, analyze their opponents' strategies, create their own strategies, and implement those strategies on the playing field. Figure 1 presents some examples of how teachers can do this in language arts, mathematics, social studies, and science.

When we use this framework, relatively few activities will end up requiring only one of these four abilities. On the contrary, most activities will be a mixture, as are the tasks we confront in everyday life. Notice that in this framework, instruction and assessment are closely related. Almost any activity that is used for the one can be used for the other.

In addition, no type of activity should be limited to students whose strength is in that area. On the contrary, we should teach all students in all four ways. In that way, each student will find at least some aspects of the instruction and assessment to be compatible with his or her preferred way of learning and other aspects to be challenging, if perhaps somewhat uncomfortable.

Teaching in all four ways also makes the teacher's job easier and more manageable. No teacher can individualize instruction and assessment for each student in a large class, but any teacher can teach in a way that meets all students' needs.

DOES THIS WORK IN PRACTICE?

In the summer of 1993, we conducted a study of high school students to test our hypothesis that students learn and perform better when they are taught in a way that at least partially matches their own strengths (Sternberg 1996; Sternberg and Clinkenbeard 1995; Sternberg et al. 1996). Known as the Yale Summer Psychology Program, the study involved 199 students from high schools across the United States and some from abroad.

Each school had nominated students for the program. Interested nominees then took a test designed to measure their analytical, creative, and practical abilities. The test included multiple-choice verbal, quantitative, and figural items, as well as analytical, creative, and practical essay items (Sternberg 1993). A sample of the items appears in Figure 2.

Figure 1
Teaching for Four Abilities
Type of Skill

	Memory	Analysis	Creativity	Practicality
Language Arts	Remember what a gerund is or what the name of Tom Sawyer's aunt was.	Compare the function of a gerund to that of a participle, or compare the personality of Tom Sawyer to that of Huckleberry Finn.	Invent a sentence that effectively uses a gerund, or write a very short story with Tom Sawyer as a character.	Find gerunds in a newspaper or magazine article and describe how they are used, or say what general lesson about persuasion can be learned from Tom Sawyer's way of persuading his friends to whitewash Aunt Polly's fence.
Mathematics	Remember a mathematical formula (Distance = Rate × Time).	Solve a mathematical word problem (using the D=RT formula).	Create your own mathematical word problem using the D=RT formula.	Show how to use the D=RT formula to estimate driving time from one city to another near you.
Social Studies	Remember a list of factors that led up to the U.S. Civil War.	Compare, contrast, and evaluate the arguments of those who supported slavery versus those who opposed it.	Write a page of a journal from the viewpoint of a soldier fighting for one or the other side during the Civil War.	Discuss the applicability of lessons of the Civil War for countries today that have strong internal divisions, such as the former Yugoslavia.
Science	Name the main types of bacteria.	Analyze the means the immune system uses to fight bacterial infections.	Suggest ways to cope with the increasing immunity bacteria are showing to antibiotic drugs.	Suggest three steps that individuals might take to reduce the likelihood of bacterial infection.

Figure 2
Sample Multiple-Choice Questions from the
Sternberg Triarchic Abilities Test

Analytical Verbal	The vip was green, so I started to cross the street. Vip most likely means:
	A. car
	B. sign
	C. light
	D. tree

Analytical
Verbal

The vip was green, so I started to cross the street. Vip most likely means:

A. car
B. sign
C. light
D. tree

Creative
Quantitative

There is a new mathematical operation called graf. It is defined as follows:

$x \text{ graf } y = x + y$, if $x < y$ but
$x \text{ graf } y = x - y$, if otherwise.
How much is 4 graf 7?

A. −3
B.   3
C. 11
D. −11

Practical
Figural
(Students are
shown a map)

After attending a performance at the theater, you need to drive to House A. If you want to avoid the traffic jam at the intersection of Spruce Avenue and Willow Street and take the shortest alternative route, you will drive

A. west on Maple Avenue to Route 326.
B. west on Pine Street to Hickory Street.
C. east on Maple Avenue to Oak Street.
D. east on Pine Street to Oak Street.

We then selected the students who fit into one of five ability patterns: high analytical, high creative, high practical, high balanced (high in all three abilities), or low balanced (low in all three abilities). We based these judgments on both the individual student's patterns and the way these patterns compared to those of the other students.

We then placed each student into one of four differentiated instructional treatments. All included a morning lecture that balanced memory, analysis, creativity, and practical learning and thinking. All students used the same introductory psychology text (Sternberg 1995), which was also balanced among the four types of learning and thinking. The treatments differed, however, in the afternoon discussion sections. There, we assigned students to a section that emphasized either memory, analysis, creativity, or practical learning and thinking.

The critical feature of this design was that, based on their ability patterns, some students were matched and others mismatched to the instructional emphasis of their section. Another important feature was that all students received at least some instruction emphasizing each type of ability.

We assessed student achievement through homework assignments, tests, and an independent project. We assessed memory specifically through multiple-choice tests, and we evaluated analytical, creative, and practical abilities through essays. For the essays, we asked students questions such as "Discuss the advantages and disadvantages of having armed guards at school" (analysis); "Describe what your ideal school would be like" (creativity); and "Describe some problem you have been facing in your life and then give a practical solution" (practical use).

Because we assessed all students in exactly the same way, we could more easily compare the groups' performance. Had we used the more conventional forms of instruction and assessment, emphasizing memory and analysis, the creative and practical ability tests would probably not have told us much.

SOME SURPRISES

The study yielded many findings, but four stand out:

1.   Students whose instruction matched their pattern of abilities performed significantly better than the others. Even by partially matching instruction to abilities, we could improve student achievement.

2.   By measuring creative and practical abilities, we significantly improved our ability to predict course performance.

3.   To our surprise, our four high-ability groups differed in their racial, ethnic, and socioeconomic composition. The high-analytic group was composed mostly of white, middle- to upper-middle-class students from well-known "good" schools. The high-creative and high-practical groups were much more diverse racially, ethnically, socioeconomically, and educationally. Our high-balanced group was in between. This pattern suggests that when we expand the range of abilities we test for, we also expand the range of students we identify as smart.

4. When we did a statistical analysis of the ability factors underlying performance on our ability test, we found no single general factor (sometimes called a *g* factor score or an IQ). This suggests that the general ability factor that has been found to underlie many conventional ability tests may not be truly general, but general only in the narrow range of abilities that conventional tests assess.

A CLEAR-EYED SENSE OF ACCOMPLISHMENT

By exposing students to instruction emphasizing each type of ability, we enable them to capitalize on their strengths while developing and improving new skills. This approach is also important because students need to learn that the world cannot always provide them with activities that suit their preferences. At the same time, if students are never presented with activities that suit them, they will never experience a sense of success and accomplishment. As a result, they may tune out and never achieve their full potential.

On a personal note, I was primarily a creative learner in classes that were largely oriented toward memorizing information. When in college, I took an introductory psychology course that was so oriented; I got a *C*, leading my instructor to suggest that I might want to consider another career path. What's more, that instructor was a psychologist who specialized in learning and memory! I might add that never once in my career have I had to memorize a book or lecture. But I have continually needed to think analytically, creatively, and practically in my teaching, writing, and research.

Success in today's job market often requires creativity, flexibility, and a readiness to see things in new ways. Furthermore, students who graduate with *A*'s, but who cannot apply what they have learned may find themselves failing on the job.

Creativity, in particular, has become even more important over time, just as other abilities have become less valuable. For example, with the advent of computers and calculators, both penmanship and arithmetic skills have diminished in importance. Some standardized ability tests, such as the SAT, even allow students to use calculators. With the increasing availability of massive, rapid data-retrieval systems, the ability to memorize information will become even less important.

This is not to say that memory and analytical abilities are not important. Students need to learn and remember the core content of the curriculum, and they need to be able to analyze—to think critically about—the material. But the importance of these abilities should not be allowed to obfuscate what else is important.

In a pluralistic society, we cannot afford to have a monolithic conception of intelligence and schooling; it's simply a waste of talent. And, as I unexpectedly found in my study, it's no random waste. The more we teach and assess students based on a broader set of abilities, the more racially, ethnically, and socioeconomically diverse our achievers will be. We can easily change our closed system—and we should. We must take a more balanced approach to education to reach all of our students.

Author's note: This research was supported under the Javits Act Program (Grant R206R50001), administered by the U.S. Department of Education's Office of Educational Research and Improvement. The findings and opinions expressed here do not reflect the Office's positions or policies.

REFERENCES

Gardner, H. (1993). *Creating Minds.* New York: Basic Books.

———. (1995). *Leading Minds.* New York: Basic Books.

Sternberg, R. J. (1993). "Sternberg Triarchic Abilities Test." Unpublished test.

———. (1994). "Diversifying Instruction and Assessment." *The Educational Forum* 59, 1: 47–53.

———. (1995). *In Search of the Human Mind.* Orlando, Fla.: Harcourt Brace College Publishers.

———. (1996). *Successful Intelligence.* New York: Simon & Schuster.

Sternberg, R. J., and P. Clinkenbeard. (May–June 1995). "A Triarchic View of Identifying, Teaching, and Assessing Gifted Children." *Roeper Review* 17, 4: 255–260.

Sternberg, R. J., M. Ferrari, P. Clinkenbeard, and E. L. Grigorenko. (1996). "Identification, Instruction, and Assessment of Gifted Children: A Construct Validation of a Triarchic Model." *Gifted Child Quarterly* 40: 129–137.

Sternberg, R. J., and L. Spear-Swerling. (1996). *Teaching for Thinking.* Washington, D.C.: American Psychological Association.

Sternberg, R. J., R. K. Wagner, W. M. Williams, and J. A. Horvath. (1995). "Testing Common Sense." *American Psychologist* 50, 11: 912–927.

Sternberg, R. J., and W. M. Williams. (1996). *How to Develop Student Creativity.* Alexandria, Va.: ASCD.

Williams, W. M., T. Blythe, N. White, J. Li, R. J. Sternberg, and H. I. Gardner. (1996). *Practical Intelligence for School: A Handbook for Teachers of Grades 5–8.* New York: HarperCollins.

Bioelectronic Learning: The Effects of Electronic Media on a Developing Brain

by Robert Sylwester

Electronic media can powerfully affect the developing brains of children and exploit the brain's analytical and response systems. But caring, enlightened parents and teachers can help avoid damage to developing minds, and lead children to achieve balance and individualism in an electronic world.

APPORTIONING TIME AND ENERGY

We have about 150,000 hours of living to expend between the ages of one and 18. We sleep about 50,000 hours of this time, and we dream about two hours of the eight we sleep each night. Sleeping and dreaming appear to be positively related to the development and maintenance of the long-term memories that emerge out of daytime activities, because they allow our brain to eliminate the interference of external sensorimotor activity while it physically adds to, edits, and erases the neural network connections that create long-term memories.

We spend about 65,000 of our 100,000 waking hours involved in solitary activities and in direct informal relationships with family and friends, activities that play a major role in the development and maintenance of important *personal* memories.

We spend about 35,000 of our waking hours with our larger culture in formal and informal metaphoric-symbolic activities—about 12,000 hours in school and about twice that much with various

From *Technos: Quarterly for Education and Technology*, vol. 6, no. 2, Summer 1997, pp. 19–22. Reprinted with permission.

forms of mass media (TV, computers, films, music, sports, non-school print media, churches, museums). Mass media and school thus play major roles in the development and maintenance of important *cultural* memories.

So on an average developmental day between the ages of one and 18, a young person sleeps eight hours and spends 10 waking hours with self, family, and friends, four hours with mass media—and only two hours in school. Our society has incredible expectations for those two hours!

Young people tend to spend much time and energy on such electronic media as video games, TV, and computers—at the expense of nonelectronic media and socialization (although new forms of socialization are evolving around watching TV and playing video games).

> **. . . this is the first generation to directly interact with and alter the content on the screen and the conversation on the radio.**

The attentional demands of electronic media range from rapt (video games) to passive (much TV), but this is the first generation to directly interact with and alter the content on the screen and the conversation on the radio. These "screenagers" emotionally understand electronic media in ways that adults don't (somewhat as a virus that replicates cultural reality, instead of as a mere communicator of events). For example, portable cameras have helped to shift TV's content from dramatic depictions to live theater that extends (and often endlessly repeats and discusses) live coverage of such breaking events as wars, accidents, trials, sports, and talk-show arguments. What occurs anywhere is immediately available everywhere. And like a virus, such events move from electronic depictions into next-day conversations everywhere. Our world has truly become a gossipy global village where everyone knows everyone else's business.

Emotion drives attention, which drives learning, memory, behavior, and just about everything else. Our brain's key emotion-driven questions when confronting something new are: do I eat it? do I run away from it? or do I mate with it?

Given the ready availability of channel changers, mass-media programmers often insert strong primal emotional elements into their programming to capture and hold attention. Since violence, sexuality, and consumerism in media trigger primal emotions, most young people confront continuous consumer-driven commercials (eat it), thousands of violent acts (run away from it), and heavy doses of sexuality (mate with it) during their childhood media interactions. This comes at the expense of other more positive and normative experiences with human behaviors and interactions. Mass media tend to show us how to be *buyers* not *producers, powerful* not *peaceful,* and *sexy* not *sexual.*

> **Mass media tend to show us how to be *buyers* not *producers, powerful* not *peaceful,* and *sexy* not *sexual.***

Commercial sponsorship in mass media has led to a distorted presentation of important cultural and consumer-related issues. For example, TV commercials tend to be short, superficial, and (understandably) factually biased. Further, computer programs and TV editing techniques tend to compress, extend, and distort normal time-space relationships, a critically important element in the creation and use of effective long-term memories. Most of our memories are context-driven, and these electronic distortions can seriously alter the natural context of the experience.

OUR BRAIN AND ELECTRONIC MEDIA: BIOLOGICAL SYSTEMS, CULTURAL ISSUES

Brain Development

Our awesomely complex yet elegantly simple brain is the best-organized three pounds of matter in the known universe. Decidedly human but individually unique, it is a wary, curious, and exploratory organ that actively experiences and interprets its environment, applying a variety of cognitive models and systems that it develops (within established limits) to the reality it perceives. The brain, as a basic animal organ, developed in three successive layers over evolutionary time to meet survival, emotional, and finally rational challenges. Our rational cortical forebrain is unique among animal brains in its size and capabilities, but our subcortical survival and emotional systems play very powerful roles in our thoughts and behavior.

Our brain is composed of tens of billions of highly interconnected neurons that interact electrochemically with surrounding and distant neurons through a complex system of tubular (dendrite/axon) extensions that receive and send messages. Cortical neurons are organized into a vast number of dedicated semiautonomous columnar modules (or networks), most of which are modifiable by the experiences that wire up our brain to it environment. Each module processes a very specific function, and groups of modules consolidate their functions to process more complex cognitive functions. So, for example, sounds become phonemes become words become sentences become stories.

Genetics plays a much larger role in brain development and capability than previously believed. Because biological evolution proceeds much slower than cultural evolution, we're born with a generic human brain that's genetically tuned more to the pastoral ecological environment that humans lived in thousands of years ago than to our fast-paced urban electronic environment.

Our curiosity and inherently strong problem-solving capabilities allowed us to develop such tools as autos, books, computers, and drugs that compensate for our body and brain limitations, and very powerful portable electronic computerized instruments are now rapidly transforming our culture. We can thus view drugs and technology as a fourth technological brain—located outside of our skull but powerfully interactive with the three integrated biological brains within our skull.

Motivation, experience, and training can enhance generic capabilities (for instance, infants can easily master any human language, but they aren't born proficient in any of them), so brain development is a dynamic mix of nature and nurture. Thus it's important to choose our parents carefully, because they provide us with our *genes* and our *jeans* (the home environment that introduces us to our culture). Done right, it's an appropriate mix of biology, technology, and society. Trying to determine whether nature or nurture is developmentally more important is like trying to determine if length or width is more important in computing area.

Our brain is designed to adapt its cortical networks to the environment in which it lives (to master the local language, for example). A socially interactive environment that stimulates curiosity and exploration enhances the development of an effective brain. Thus excessive childhood involvement with electronic media that limit social interaction could hinder the development of a brain's social systems. Conversely, denying a child easy and extensive exploration of electronic technology helps to create an electronically hampered adult in an increasingly electronic culture. Surfing on the Internet (or on anything else electronic) is the screenagers' version of beginning the process of learning how to drive a car by first getting on a tricycle.

Memory Systems

Our short-term (or working) memory is an attentional buffer that allows us to hold a few units of information for a short period while we determine their importance. Since the system has space-time limitations, it must rapidly combine (or chunk) key related bits of foreground information into single units by identifying similarities/differences/patterns that can simplify an otherwise confusing sensory field. The appeal of computerized video games may well lie in their lack of explicit instructions to the players, who suddenly find themselves in complex electronic environments that challenge them to quickly identify and act on rapidly changing elements that may or may not be important. Failure sends the player back to the beginning, and success brings a more complex albeit attractive challenge in the next electronic environment.

> The appeal of computerized video games may well lie in their lack of explicit instructions to the players . . .

Our short-term memory processes *frame* the segment of the environment that we perceive. We attend to the things that are inside the frame, and we're merely aware of the context, the things that are outside of the frame. Mass media often eliminate a proper presentation of the context of an event and so distort its meaning and importance. The result is that a rare isolated event is presented as being common. A brutal murder in a park may empty all the parks in a large region. Parents and teachers must help children to develop a sense of the context of the electronic media world they experience. Unfortunately, too many adults equate rare with common if the event is emotionally charged, considering *data* to be the plural of *anecdote,* as it were.

The efficiency of our dual long-term memory system depends on our ability to string together and access long sequences of related motor actions into automatic skills (procedural memory) and related objects/events into stories (declarative memory). Thus *storytelling* activities dominate our culture through such communicative devices as conversations, jokes, songs, novels, films, TV, ballets, and sports. Young people must master various storytelling forms and techniques, and electronic media can both help and hinder this process through their range, editing techniques, and interactive potential.

Response Systems

Our brain uses two systems to analyze and respond to environmental challenges, and electronic mass media often exploit them. One is a relatively slow, analytic, reflective system (thalamus-hippocampus-cortex circuitry) that explores the more objective factual elements of a situation, compares them with related declarative memories, and then responds. It's best suited to nonthreatening situations that don't require an instant response—life's little challenges. It often functions through storytelling forms and sequences and so is tied closely to our language and classification capabilities. User-friendly computer programs and nonfrantic TV programming tend to activate this rational system. The other one is a fast, conceptual, reflexive system (thalamus-amygdala-cerebellum-stress circuitry) that identifies the fearful and survival elements in a situation and quickly activates automatic response patterns (procedural memory) if survival seems problematic. This fast system developed to respond to imminent predatory danger and fleeting feeding and mating opportunities (eat/run/mate). It thus focuses on any loud, looming, contrasting, moving, obnoxious, or attractive elements that signal potential danger, food, or mates.

> ... chronic activation of the fear pathways can result in physical deterioration within our memory systems.

The system thus enhances survival, and so it's the default system. But its rapid superficial analysis often leads us to respond fearfully, impulsively, and inappropriately to situations that didn't require an immediate response. Stereotyping and prejudice are but two of the prices we humans continually pay for this powerful survival system. Regrets and apologies run a close second. Worse, the neurotransmitter or hormonal discharges associated with fear can strengthen the emotional and weaken the factual memories of an event if the stressful situation is serious or chronic. We've become fearful of something, but we're not sure why, so we've learned little from the experience that's consciously useful. LeDoux (1996) discovered that chronic activation of the fear pathways can result in physical deterioration within our memory systems.

All that is serious business, because people often use mass media to exploit this system by stressing elements that trigger rapid irrational fear responses. Politicians demonize opponents; sales pitches demand an immediate response; zealots focus on fear of groups who differ from their definition of acceptable. The fingernail-size amygdala, the area of the brain that triggers this system, has appropriately been called the fear button.

The fast pacing of TV and video-game programming and their focus on bizarre/violent/sexual elements also trigger this system. If the audience perceives these elements and the resulting visceral responses as the real-world norm, the electronic media must continually escalate the bizarre/violent/sexual behavior to trigger the fast system. Rational thought development would thus suffer. Those who are still looking can now see this escalation in the mass media.

Conversely, if a person perceives these electronic-world elements as an aberration and not normative of the real world, such electronic experiences can often actually help to develop rational thought and appropriate response. Those who understand the normative center of a phenomenon must also know about its outer reaches—and mass media provide a useful metaphoric format for observing the outer reaches of something without actually experiencing it (an escape, for instance, from a dangerous situation one might confront).

So perhaps it's not what electronic media bring to a developing mind that's most important but rather what the developing mind brings to the electronic media. Children who mature in a secure home and school with adults who explore all the dimensions of humanity in a nonhurried, accepting atmosphere can probably handle most electronic media without damaging their dual memory and response systems. They will tend to delay their responses, to look deeper than the surface of things. Furthermore, they will probably also prefer to spend much more of their time in direct interactions with real people. They will thus develop the sense of balance that permits them to be a part of the real electronic worlds—but also to stand apart from them.

FURTHER READING

Chen, Milton. 1994. *Smart Parents' Guide to Children's TV*. San Francisco: KQED Books/Tapes.

Diamond, Marian. 1988. *Enriching Heredity: The Impact of the Environment on the Anatomy of the Brain*. New York: Free Press.

Educational Leadership. 1994. Theme issue, "Realizing the Promise of Technology," April.

Greenfield, Patricia. 1984. *Mind and Media: The Effects of Television, Video Games, and Computers*. Cambridge, Mass.: Harvard University Press.

Healy, Jane. 1990. *Endangered Minds: Why Children Don't Think and What We Can Do About It*. New York: Simon and Schuster.

LeDoux, Joseph. 1996. *The Emotional Brain: The Mysterious Underpinnings of Emotional Life*. New York: Simon and Schuster.

Provenzio, Eugene. 1991. *Video Kids: Making Sense of Nintendo*. Cambridge, Mass.: Harvard University Press.

Rushkoff, Douglas. 1994. *Media Virus: Hidden Agendas in Popular Culture*. New York: Ballantine.

Schank, Roger. 1990. *Tell Me a Story: A New Look at Real and Artificial Memory*. New York: Simon and Schuster.

Sylwester, Robert. 1995. *A Celebration of Neurons: An Educator's Guide to the Human Brain*. Alexandria, Va.: Association for Supervision and Curriculum Development.

Sylwester, Robert. 1990. "Expanding the Range, Dividing the Task; Educating the Human Brain in an Electronic Society," *Educational Leadership*, October.

Turkle, Sherry. 1995. *Life on the Screen: Identity in the Age of the Internet*. New York: Simon and Schuster.

West, Thomas. 1991. *In the Mind's Eye: Visual Thinkers, Gifted People with Learning Difficulties, Computer Images, and the Ironies of Creativity*. Buffalo, N.Y.: Prometheus.

Forecasts for Technology in Education

by David Moursund

The future of information technology in education is harder to forecast than the general future of information technology. One difficulty is that students and teachers do not control the school budget. As pointed out by Seymour Sarason (1990), they lack power. Another difficulty is that education does not easily change. It is a complex social system. For these reasons, the forecasts or predictions that follow are made with somewhat limited confidence.

But by and large, the forecasts are optimistic. They are forecasts of our educational system effectively coping with the changes being wrought by technology. They are forecasts of students getting a better education. Many of these ideas were previously discussed in Moursund (1992).

ELEVEN GENERAL FORECASTS

Following are brief discussions of 11 different forecasts for information technology in education. In many ways, these are linked to the general goals for information technology in education. In essence, we are in a situation where the underlying science and technology make it technically possible to achieve these goals. There are a number of underlying driving forces that are contributing to schools adopting some or all of the goals. The commitment of resources, if it continues to grow, will cause these forecasts to be accurate.

Adapted from *The Future of Information Technology in Education,* by David Moursund, chapter 7, pp. 77–87. © 1997 by International Society for Technology in Education. All rights reserved. Reprinted with permission.

Student Access to Computing Power

The total amount of computing power available to students is growing quite rapidly, and this growth will continue for many years to come. The growth comes from two main sources:

1.   The number of microcomputers in schools and in the homes of students is continuing to increase. Eventually the great majority of students will have routine access to a portable microcomputer that they carry between home and school. These portables will have easy to use interfaces with more powerful microcomputers that schools will make available to their students.

2.   The capabilities of the microcomputers available to students are increasing at a rapid pace.

In the United States at the current time, schools have approximately one microcomputer per eight students. However, there are a number of school sites in which the ratio is approximately one microcomputer per student, or even better. The number of such sites will increase relatively rapidly during the next decade.

Connectivity

The megatrend toward providing students and teachers with connections to the computer networks of the world is well underway. Increasingly, educational leaders and policy makers agree that students should have connectivity to other students within and beyond the school building, and to the information sources of the world.

There is considerable agreement that libraries will become "virtual libraries"—that is, that library contents will be distributed electronically throughout the world, rather than being physically available only in isolated buildings. Such libraries will be accessible to students both in the classroom and at home. This represents a major change in the world. Already, students of all ages are learning how to make effective use of libraries that previously had only been available to a select few researchers.

The pace of increased connectivity is faster in the business world than it is in the home market. It is faster in the home market than it is in schools. When all three markets are taken together, it seems clear that both our formal and our informal educational systems will experience continued rapid growth in connectivity for many years to come. In terms of the S-shaped growth curve, we are beginning to enter a time of very rapid growth. It appears that this period of rapid growth will extend over many years.

Of course, there is a substantial difference between providing schools with the connectivity and thoroughly integrating effective use of this connectivity into the curriculum. The needed investment in teacher training and curriculum development will be slow in coming. Teacher training remains a major impediment to the rapid increase of effective use of information technology in schools.

> **Teacher training remains a major impediment to the rapid increase of effective use of information technology in school.**

Artificial Intelligence

Computers will continue to get "smarter." That is, they will grow in their capability of doing intelligent-like things. More and more problems will be solved by merely expressing the problem in a format that fits the computer's capabilities. Increasingly, the human-machine interface will make it easier to do this, and the interface itself will make use of results developed by the field of artificial intelligence.

There are now thousands of expert systems in everyday use. These systems are computer programs based on past successful solutions to particular problems. They have a level of "intelligence" adequate to help accomplish tasks and solve problems within a narrow scope. Such expert systems are "fragile"—that is, they only perform well within the narrow domains they were designed for. This means that people using such expert systems have to have a good knowledge both of the domain of the expert system and how to recognize a problem outside of that domain.

The capabilities of such expert systems will continue to increase. They provide excellent examples of where a person and a computer who are trained to work together can outperform either working individually.

Problems will increasingly be solved by teams composed of humans, computers, and computerized equipment such as robots and automated factories. It takes considerable knowledge and experience for a human to be an effective member of such a team. The capabilities of two of the team members (the computer and the automated equipment) will continue to increase rapidly. This places an added burden on the human member of the team. The human provides a unifying sense of purpose and perspective, and defines the overall task and the goals. This role is indispensable.

Education is faced by the problem of educating people to become integral members of the three-part team consisting of humans, computers, and automated equipment. This is not an easy educational task; it is one that our educational system has so far done little to address. In many cases the human component of this three-part team will, itself, be a team. Our schools have made substantial progress in cooperative learning—teams of students learning to learn together. Far less progress is occurring in helping students gain skills in collaborative problem solving.

> Eventually schools will take it for granted that reading and writing mean both the conventional paper-based and also hypermedia-based activities.

Other aspects of artificial intelligence will have a profound impact on education. Voice input provides an example. Already, voice input is widely used in the commercial world. Educators have little insight into how to teach reading and writing in an environment that includes high-quality voice input and voice output systems.

Hypermedia

Hypermedia is an interactive environment that includes text, color, voice, sound, graphics, and video. Hypermedia allows user interactivity in the information retrieval process. Users can choose individual pathways through information collections, and the information itself can be presented in multiple formats that better fit the needs of individual users. Increasingly, information is being stored in a hypermedia format, and this trend will continue.

Schools are embarking on a pathway in which all students will become proficient in reading (that is, using) hypermedia. Students are learning to retrieve information stored on CD-ROMs, in hypermedia computer files, in computerized databases, and on the Internet's World Wide Web. Eventually such electronic access to hypermedia-based information will be commonplace.

Schools are also embarking on a pathway of having students learn to write (create) hypermedia documents. The trend is clear. Eventually schools will take it for granted that reading and writing mean both the conventional paper-based and also hypermedia-based activities. However, interactivity, sound, color, still photography, computer-based drawing and painting, and video add new dimensions to communication. In total, facilitating students in developing basic skills in reading and writing hypermedia will prove to be a major challenge to our educational system. Given the limited resources and time that teachers have for acquiring and integrating these new skills themselves, schools will probably be slow to provide extensive hypermedia learning opportunities to students.

This will tend to create a situation in which some students become facile at reading and writing hypermedia, while other students develop only a reading skill in this area. As the hypermedia literate students progress through our school system, they will present a major challenge to their teachers. For example, if a teacher lacks skills in writing hypermedia, how will the teacher adequately assess the work of students that is presented in this format? How will the teacher help such students increase their skills in communicating in hypermedia?

Productivity Tools for Students

The generic and specialized computer productivity tools for adults will continue to get better and will become better interconnected. Increasingly, similar tools will be integrated into the content of the K–12 curriculum. Students will grow up using the computer productivity tools of adults. Curriculum content will reflect the capability of these productivity tools.

Curriculum content and tools used to solve problems and accomplish the tasks of a discipline have always been interwoven. This will continue as computers become commonplace in the schools. Thus, we will see substantial changes in the content of the various disciplines. Some will be more affected than others, depending on how powerful the computer tool is in each particular discipline.

Because of the pace of change of overall computer capability, there will be an increased pace of change of curriculum content. The content will adjust to the capabilities of computers as an aid to solving the problems and accomplishing the tasks of the discipline.

We already see this, for example, in accounting and graphic arts coursework. The advanced math curriculum in high schools is increasingly being driven by the capabilities of handheld graphing calculators. Eventually this calculator-driven curriculum will become a computer-driven curriculum. Because students are not limited to problems easily solved with pencil and paper, they can approach more sophisticated content earlier in their educational careers. Similar statements hold for science courses—especially those that make substantial use of mathematics.

Progress in thoroughly integrating student productivity tools into the curriculum will be slow. It requires substantial investments in teacher training, curriculum development, and the assessment system. All three of these areas of needed capacity building are currently underfunded and will continue to be underfunded.

Teacher Productivity Tools

Many different computer tools can help increase teacher productivity. Examples include word processor, electronic gradebook, databases of exam questions, lesson plans stored in a word processor, and so on. Access to the Web gives teachers access to subject matter information and lesson plans. There has been and will continue to be a steady increase in teacher use of such productivity tools.

There is a different class of teacher productivity tools—ones that may enhance student learning and teacher effectiveness. These are the desktop presentation tools and other electronic aids to teachers interacting both with students and the curriculum in a classroom setting. We can expect substantial growth in use of teacher productivity tools.

For example, a classroom can have Internet connectivity. During a discussion between students and the teacher, either the students or the teacher may retrieve information from remote databases or from people. This type of classroom computer use is now in its infancy; it will grow rapidly in years to come.

As a second example, consider a package of mathematics software that the students are learning to use. With appropriate desktop presentation projection equipment and a computer, the teacher can interact with the whole class or with small groups of students, demonstrating key features of the software. Samples of student work can be displayed and discussed. Students and teacher can work together to explore problems, making use of the computer capabilities.

A third example is provided by having students and teachers interact electronically. Assignments and materials can be provided to students through this electronic highway. Questions can be asked and answered. Assignments can be submitted and then returned electronically.

Finally, consider computer-assisted learning (CAL) and other aids to student learning. Teacher productivity can be increased by relegating certain instructional tasks to such facilities.

Technology-Enhanced Learning

Several of the components of computer use as an aid to learning
are coming together to form a combination we call technology-
enhanced learning (TEL). TEL consists of:

    1.   The combination of computer-assisted learning (with
built-in computer-managed instruction [CMI]), distance education,
and electronic access to both information and people.

    2.   Aids to teacher interactivity with students and student
interactivity with each other, such as desktop presentation, email,
and groupware.

    3.   Increasingly powerful student productivity tools with
built-in learning aids, context sensitive help, templates, and other
aids to producing high-quality products. These help a user to learn
while doing.

    Via TEL, more and more education will take place at a time and
place that is convenient to the needs of the learner. Convenient education is a megatrend in formal and informal education.

    "Just-in-time" education is a second aspect to this TEL trend.
Some learning tasks take years; it is not possible to master a second
language just at the point you need to communicate in it. However,
many other learning tasks can be completed in a few minutes, a few
hours, or a few days—just in time to apply the skills when needed.
How rapidly and effectively the learning occurs depends on the
background and capabilities of the learner and on the learning environment. Our educational system needs to help students gain increased skill in being "just-in-time" learners. This is an important
component of learning to learn and being a lifetime learner.

    A third aspect of TEL can be found in the changing capability of
the informal educational system. Almost all general-purpose home
computers that people purchase today come equipped with a CD-
ROM drive. Microsoft's Windows '95 operating system contains
built-in support of telecommunications. The trend is clear. Technology-enhanced information access will allow homes, businesses, and
other informal education environments increasingly to support just-
in-time and convenient education. As the amount and quality of
convenient education materials continues to increase, there is the
potential that more and more of the traditional content of formal
education will be learned in informal educational settings. The role
of formal education—and of the teacher—will change.

We can get a glimpse into potential changes by asking ourselves what the unique characteristics are of a human "live" teacher, as contrasted with CAL, CMI, distance education, and other electronic aids to learning. While there are many answers, several of the most important ones are:

1. The human-human interface. This is far better than any current human-machine interface. Teachers can know their students and interact with them in a manner appropriate to the needs of human beings.

2. The versatility of the human teacher. A human teacher can facilitate an interdisciplinary discussion that ranges over whatever comes to the minds of the students and the teacher. The human teacher has flexibility and capabilities that far exceed those of any current computer system in this regard.

3. The social aspects of education. Education is a social activity. Human teachers, along with the interactions among students and with teachers, are essential to our formal and informal educational system.

This type of analysis suggests that our formal educational system will place more of its structured efforts into making effective use of the uniquely human characteristics and strengths of human teachers. More of the subject matter content and rote skill components of the curriculum will be left to TEL.

Curriculum Content

Increasingly, computers can solve or help solve the types of problems that students study in school. The usefulness of computers as an aid to problem solving cuts across all academic disciplines. However, computers are far more useful in some disciplines than others. For example, while computers are useful tools in both art and music, they are more central to accounting, mathematics, and science.

To date, the content of the K–12 curriculum has not changed a great deal due to computer technology. We have previously mentioned the growing role of calculators in mathematics instruction, and the toehold of the microcomputer-based laboratory in science education. The use of computer simulations and simulation games is slowly growing. Through the use of such simulations, individual students or a whole class can explore complex problem-solving situations in business, science, and social science.

Another example is provided by students learning to use electronic aids to retrieving information. Instruction in the electronic accessing of information is replacing instruction in non-electronic ways to access information. It is now clear that all students need to develop some of the information retrieval skills of a research librarian. Instruction in such skills can begin at the primary school level.

> It is now clear that all students need to develop some of the information retrieval skills of a research librarian.

We will see a slow but steady change in the content of all academic curriculum areas due to information technology. The pace of this change will accelerate as computer facilities become more readily available to students and teachers, and as each group becomes more skilled in their use.

Preservice Education of Teachers

The National Council for Accreditation of Teacher Education (NCATE) is the main accreditation agency for Colleges of Education in the United States. NCATE is making continuing progress toward accreditation standards that will require both preservice teachers and their faculty to become computer literate. This is a trend that will continue.

More and more preservice teachers have had a number of years of computer experience while they were in the K–12 educational system. Thus, the average level of computer knowledge of preservice teachers is steadily increasing. This trend will continue.

Taken together, these two trends ensure that there will be a continuing increase in the computer knowledge and skills of graduates of teacher training programs. However, this steady improvement needs to be compared against the steadily increasing capabilities of information technology in education. Right now, there is a huge gap between the needed knowledge and skills of recently graduated teachers, and their actual knowledge of computers in education. It appears likely that this gap will continue to exist—indeed, it seems likely that it will grow.

Inservice Teacher Education

One way to talk about a particular specialized education is to quantify its "half life." Suppose that a person gains the knowledge and skills to be fully qualified as a neurosurgeon or a cardiologist. Suppose that this person then gains no new knowledge or skills, while the contemporary standards continue to increase. How many years will it be before this person is only "half qualified"? While such a quantification is not particularly scientific, it does provide a basis for analysis and discussion. The half life of a neurosurgeon or a cardiologist might be in the range of three to four years.

> Information technology is affecting both the content and the pedagogy of every discipline at every teaching level.

What is the half life of a teacher's education? How is it affected by the rapid pace of change in the totality of human knowledge or by changes in technology? Although we do not have precise answers, it is clear that the rapid pace of change in technology has greatly shortened the half life of a teacher's education.

At one time, it was common for teachers to obtain lifetime teaching certificates. In more recent years, most states have put in requirements that a teacher have some continuing teaching experience and a certain amount of coursework or other training for certificate renewal.

Information technology in education has added a new and perplexing dimension to this picture. Information technology is affecting both the content and the pedagogy of every discipline at every teaching level. Moreover, it is not easy to develop the needed knowledge and skills effectively to integrate the technology into the everyday curriculum. The facility with which some students pick up technology skills often serves to increase pressure on the educator, as traditional roles of teacher and learner are disrupted.

Our inservice teacher education system was not designed to deal with a rapid pace of change. It is proving inadequate in dealing with computer-based technology. Unless there is a major restructuring in our inservice education system, there will be a growing gap between the potentials of information technology in education and the actual implementation. At the current time, there is little indication that the needed restructuring of our inservice education system is occurring.

The analysis of preservice and inservice teacher education leads to a forecast of a continuing major gap between information technology knowledge and skills needed by teachers and their actual knowledge and skills.

The School-Home Connection

Computers and connectivity are having a significant impact on the "home" part of our formal and informal educational system. Current estimates are that close to half of the school children in this country have access to a computer at home. This suggests that there are 4 to 5 times as many computers in the homes of school age children as there are in our schools. It also means that there is substantial inequity in students having access to the technology. Those students who come from a home situation where there is a computer and parents who know how to make effective use of a computer may be receiving several times as much instruction and experience with computers as those students from other homes.

The following two news items suggest that computers and connectivity will continue to grow in the homes of school age children.

Education is Key to Home PC Market

An American Learning Household Survey says that over 80% of intended family household PC buyers in its study cited children's education as the primary reason for purchase, relegating work-at-home and home financial applications to a distant 40% level. The survey also found that children's use of the PC is shifting away from games and toward more complex uses of the computer as an information access tool.

(The Red Herring Dec 95)

Sega Will Add Browser to Gaming Equipment

Sega Enterprises plans to add equipment to its Saturn video game console that will enable consumers to browse the Internet on their TV set. The entire package would cost between $100 and $150 more than the current $299 Saturn price tag.

(Investor's Business Daily 16 Feb 96 A30)

The news items about Sega Enterprises is especially interesting, as it suggests that we may move rapidly toward integration of entertainment and non-entertainment systems. The computing power in a game machine rivals or exceeds that in many of the general purpose microcomputers. Such computing power can be used for more than just playing games.

Educational software developers are well aware that there is both a school market and a home market for their software. Increasingly, these developers have come to realize that the home market may exceed the school market.

Of course, the home and the school markets for educational software are by no means the same. The term *edutainment* has been developed to describe software that has a combined educational and entertainment focus. If an educational product is being developed primarily for the home market, the entertainment components may well dominate over the educational components. There is relatively little solid research to support the educational value of many of the educational games that are widely sold to parents and children.

CONCLUSIONS AND RECOMMENDATION

As you make use of the educational technology forecasts discussed here, keep in mind that they are mainly forecasts based on expert opinion. Each forecast represents a potential—something that schools could be doing right now. One can summarize these forecasts by asserting that student and teacher goals for information technology will eventually be achieved. These goals will help guide our educational system over the next few decades.

The forecasts have a unifying theme—moving from first-order effects to second-order effects. Some schools and school districts will move much faster than others. However, it seems clear that our educational system as a whole is going to move toward the second-order effects, and then beyond them.

These will produce substantial disruptions in our current educational system. The planning and change process needs to be given careful attention.

RECOMMENDED READINGS

Gardner, Howard. *Extraordinary Minds: Portraits of Four Exceptional Individuals and an Examination of Our Own Extraordinariness.* New York: Basic Books, 1996.
Gardner explores his theory through the lives of four people whose achievements were extraordinary: Mozart, who totally mastered his field; Sigmund Freud, who created a new field; Virginia Woolf, who took ordinary things into the realm of the extraordinary; and Gandhi, who profoundly influenced others. Gardner takes us with him on a fascinating search for traits shared by all four, and the meaning that might have for the rest of us is fascinating.

Greenspan, Stanley. *The Growth of the Mind and the Endangered Origins of Intelligence.* Reading, MA: Addison-Wesley, 1997.
An excellent, easily read discussion of the stages of intellectual development that a child experiences and the dangers faced along the way. Strongly recommended for parents and educators.

Moursund, David. *The Future of Information Technology in Education.* Eugene, OR: International Society for Technology in Education, 1997.
Moursund is a widely recognized authority on the use of computers in education. This book provides educators with an excellent sense of current issues and directions. (Phone 541-346-2401 for information on this and other excellent ISTE publications.)

Perkins, David. *Outsmarting IQ: The Emerging Science of Learnable Intelligence.* New York: Free Press, 1995.
A superb nontechnical synthesis of current intelligence theory and research. Perkins examines current theories and proposes a practical synthesis that most educators will find appealing.

Sternberg, Robert. *Successful Intelligence: How Practical and Creative Intelligence Determine Success in Life.* New York: Simon and Schuster, 1996.
Sternberg's most recent discussion of his triarchic mind model. A very readable book with many practical suggestions.

New Perspectives on Computational Thought Processes

An important property of our brain is its ability to rapidly translate the natural space/time world into verbal sounds and line segments that communicate meaning—qualities and quantities. Thus, space becomes objects that become nouns that have adjective qualities. Similarly, time becomes events that become verbs that have adverb qualities. Prepositions provide these concepts with space/time positions (under, within, above; before, during, after) and conjunctions combine and separate the concepts.

We apparently have innate abilities in many areas that get us started in life but that then require instruction and effort to go beyond that basic level to the normal reach of human ability. We then tend to use technologies to go beyond that level (or are impressed by virtuoso performance that goes beyond normality). Thus, an innate ability to crawl, walk, and run can be extended by instruction into such more specialized movement activities as tap dancing, high jumping, and sprinting. Finally, technologies such as ice skates, bicycles, and cars move us in ways that legs alone could never hope to do.

The development of verbal and numerical computational skills is an important element of the curriculum, and we've long noted the existence of the same processing sequence of innate to learned to technologically augmented. Children under two can recognize and make speech sounds that they later learn to turn into articulate language with its various specializations (such as reading and spelling). Technologies, such as books, papers and pencils, word processors with spell checkers, and e-mail, allow us to go beyond personal face-to-face communication. Similarly, recent research suggests that very young children seem to have an innate numerical processing ability up to the quantity of three or four. Most can mentally master basic computations, such as the multiplication tables up to 12, during their elementary school years. Beyond that, though, we tend to opt for paper/pencil or calculator technologies.

This final section explores the exciting discoveries and serious challenges of understanding verbal and numerical computation. Two articles focus on scientists (Sereno and Dehaene) who are studying the neurobiology of language and mathematics. The articles show them as human beings who are struggling to solve two difficult scientific problems, and so they provide us with a sense of the move from notion to speculation to discovery in science. The other two articles focus on the need for such research. They describe the problems confronted today by students with learning disabilities—who can't wait a decade for the solution to their problems—and educators who are trying to use developments in brain theory and research to understand and then shape appropriate curricular materials and instructional practices.

These final four articles dramatically describe the challenge you and other educators face in the years ahead. While it is interesting to read what others have done and are doing, the more important question is What will you do now that you know what needs to be done?

A Brain That Talks

by Jo Ann C. Gutin

Our brains are much like those of our primate cousins, so where did
we get our uniquely human gift of speech? One human says we simply
rewired brain structures devoted to a different, more general primate
specialty—vision.

"I always had this weird idea that I had to know lots of different
things," says a faintly uncomfortable Marty Sereno. He shifts
in his chair, turning his back to a Post-it-fringed computer
screen and a table so deep in open journals that it looks like the
cross-bedded planes of a geologic formation. Sereno is sitting in his
office at the University of California at San Diego, where drawn
mini-blinds shut out the distracting southern California sunshine.
"When you're trying to do interdisciplinary stuff," he continues,
"it's no good putting two specialists together in a room, because they
can't talk to each other. You've got to pretend you're *in* the other
field; you have to go and live with the natives. It has to be all in one
head."

To understate the case considerably, the 40-year-old Sereno has
a lot of things in one head. There is his primary research interest, of
course, which is the neurological architecture of vision in primates
and rodents. Then there are the new techniques in brain imaging
that he has helped pioneer, and the computer programs he and his
collaborators have conceived to display the results. There is, as well,
a wealth of information on subjects as various as linguistics, communication systems in animals, philosophy, and modern jazz (he's an
avid guitarist).

And then there is his unconventional theory about brain evolution and the origins of human language, which has been simmering on a back burner of his mind since graduate school. The theory appears flamboyantly interdisciplinary and complex. But Sereno merely shrugs at that characterization. "Some things just have a lot of parts," he says. "Not an impossible number, but enough that ten won't do. Sometimes it just has to be a hundred."

Reduced to almost haiku proportions, Sereno's idea is this: language ability arose in the human brain not through the development of a new, uniquely human language organ, as most accounts have it, but by "a relatively minor rewiring" of a neural system that was already there. And that neural wiring belonged largely to the visual system, a part of the brain that recent research—including Sereno's own—has shown to be almost unimaginably complex.

These are statements slightly less heretical than those an earlier Martin nailed to the door of Wittenberg Castle Church, but not by much. Language is often regarded as a cognitive boundary, one of the last things that separate us from our primate cousins. But if Sereno is right, and language rode into our brains on the coattails, so to speak, of vision, we humans are once again a little less special than we thought.

For the moment, the evidence Sereno produces to support his theory is largely circumstantial; he cites chiefly the path taken by the brain in the course of its evolution. Roughly 500 million years ago, when the first vertebrates appeared, a small lump at the rear of the brain stem expanded to become the cerebellum. At the same time, a pair of small, primitive structures surrounding the brain stem and cerebellum expanded into the two hemispheres of the cerebrum. Finally, between 200 and 300 million years ago, the six-layered cerebral cortex appeared in mammals as a blanket of nerve cells covering the cerebrum. In humans, this eighth-of-an-inch-thick layer is folded in intricate wrinkles, and the rear two-thirds of it is divided into areas corresponding to the senses, or what neuroscientists call modalities: hearing, touch, vision, and so on.

As Sereno points out, we know that in the other, nonhuman higher primates, the visual processing system takes up half the cortex. It is not known precisely how much of the human brain is given over to vision—the kinds of invasive experiments traditionally needed to determine that can only be done in animals, not people. But Sereno thinks it likely that new techniques in brain scanning will reveal that we, too, have that much visual cortex in our brains. And he thinks that natural selection could well have jury-rigged those preexisting structures to perform some new functions. What could be more logical, he asks, than running the new train of language on the old tracks of vision? "We ought to pay more attention to the things animals do that might have been built upon" for language, he says. "Look—the system is definitely souped up in us. People can do a lot more stuff than monkeys can. But the basic hardware is not that different."

According to the prevailing notion of how the human brain is organized, language is centered in a couple of areas on the left side of the brain that are named for the nineteenth-century scientists who discovered them. One, called Broca's area, sits just below the temple; it is involved in language *production*. The other, Wernicke's area, is just behind the ear and seems to control language *comprehension*.

> "Look—the system is definitely souped up in us. People can do a lot more stuff than monkeys can. . . ."

Broca's and Wernicke's areas are certainly involved with language, says Sereno; his quarrel is with the idea that language is confined there. In his view, localizing a higher-order function such as language to two quarter-size patches of cortex smacks of a prescientific mindset. "It's sort of like a holdover from the phrenologists," he says, referring to proponents of the eighteenth-century notion that such individual traits as musical ability or a tendency toward violence could be detected from bumps on the skull. Sereno thinks instead that language centers might be scattered all over the brain, largely in the mosaic of cortical areas devoted to visual processing but also in parts devoted to motor coordination and auditory perception.

Most scenarios of language evolution tend to sidestep the knotty issue of what might have gone on in the human brain to make language possible. Since the researchers who are interested in language evolution tend to be linguists and anthropologists, not neuroscientists, they focus on questions such as when language evolved or what its early phases might have been like. But Sereno brings a much broader perspective to the table.

The eclecticism that has flowered into Sereno's language theory has deep roots. His mother is an artist and art teacher. His father is a former civil engineer whose heart always really belonged to psychol-

ogy and philosophy; he quit his job to become a mail carrier when
Sereno was a teenager. The two gave Martin, their oldest child, the
middle name Irenaeus, after a theologian of the second century.

Martin isn't the only family member possessed by a thirst to
know things. His brother, Paul, is a paleontologist specializing in
dinosaurs; two of his four sisters are
psycholinguists, the others neuroscientists.
"Thanksgiving dinners at our house are
pretty weird," he says. "When you get
together with your siblings, you tend to
revert to childhood anyway, but we have all
this new stuff to fight about!"

**If the mental tasks
were so similar, why
couldn't the brain be
using some of the
same wiring?**

Sereno has been casting his academic net
wide for years. After majoring in geology in
college, and uncertain what interest to pursue, he fired off applications to graduate programs in anthropology, geology, linguistics,
philosophy, and paleontology before settling on an interdisciplinary
program at the University of Chicago. The program required students to complete a master's degree in a hands-on scientific discipline as a grounding for more theoretical doctoral research. Sereno
chose neurobiology and began a project that involved mapping the
brains of turtles. (A reminder of those days, a pancake-size turtle
named Spanky, lives in an aquarium in the Serenos' kitchen.)

But he continued studying linguistics and philosophy along
with brain biology, and late one night in 1980 those disparate strands
began to twist together in the idea that the visual system might be a
pathway to language. At the time, for one paper, he'd been reviewing
the evidence that mammals have several separate brain areas devoted
to vision; simultaneously he was writing another paper on the grammar of sign language. In his spare time, meanwhile, he was doodling
mentally about the concept of codes: sign language as one kind of
code, spoken language as another, DNA as a code that tells cells what
proteins to make.

"It all jarred me loose into thinking about language in a more
general way," Sereno says. He began to see a similarity between what
the mysterious language system in the brain was doing as it tacked
together the meaning extracted from individual words in a series,
and what the visual system was doing as it put together the information gathered from a series of glances. If the mental tasks were so
similar, why couldn't the brain be using some of the same wiring?

When we look at a scene, Sereno explains, we feel as though we're taking it all in at once, but what actually happens is quite different: We scan a scene with a long series of staccato eye fixations, called saccades, which occur at a rate of several per second. Each individual saccade projects a new part of the external scene onto the retina, the network of light-sensitive cells at the back of the eyeball. The optic nerve carries that image (after a quick stop-off in a part of the brain called the dorsal lateral geniculate nucleus) to the "primary visual area," in the back of the cortex.

The image received by the primary visual area is a sort of distorted map of differences in the intensity of the light that falls on the retina. Some researchers have called this map the primal sketch. The sketch is then shuttled forward in the brain to a number of higher-order visual areas, each of which specializes in analyzing one of its aspects—color, say, or motion or form—although there appears to be a fair degree of overlap in their functions. In monkeys there are between 20 and 30 visual areas, and Sereno thinks there are probably about that many in people too. These visual areas of the brain knit the threads of the scene together, reconstructing it as a collection of objects with volume that occupy space.

"The main job of the visual part of the brain is looking around and updating some kind of representation of the world," Sereno explains, "for the purpose of getting around in it." The job of the language part of the brain is very similar, he says, except for the obvious difference that language can deal with what isn't there—the past and the future, the imagined—as well as what *is* there, in the present.

Individual words, Sereno thinks, are like individual saccades, each revealing only part of the "fictive scene." The brain of a speaker produces a string of these words in a specific order governed by the rules of syntax; the brain of a listener collects the individual words in a short-term memory storehouse, where it attempts to fit them together until enough have accumulated to create a mental picture. "Without the stuff around it," Sereno says, "you can't get much information out of a single glance. Understanding a scene requires putting together a piece of information you get ten glances down the road with one you got ten glances ago. That's very much like language, where you have a sequence of words, and then you refer with a pronoun to something that happened earlier in the sentence.

"Suppose you said, 'John went to the store. Then he went home.' A person listening to you would assume that the pronoun *he*, the guy who went home, is the same person you were referring to initially, the one who went to the store. You have the same problem in vision all the time. For example, when I glance around the room, I look at the door, I look at Bill the monkey, I look at my bicycle over there, and I look back at Bill the monkey. That's a very similar situation: you have to figure out that's the same Bill, the same monkey you were looking at before. Has Bill changed? Has Bill's relationship to other things in the scene changed?"

Sereno believes both kinds of decoding take place in the visual areas of the cortex. "When someone's speaking to you," he says, "words generate a stream of patterns in your auditory cortex. Somehow those patterns, which are representations of speech sounds, are recognized in groups that stand for words. And somehow they travel to your visual cortex and activate a little glop—a glancelike portion—of higher visual cortex activity over there. They simulate what would happen if you actually saw something." Of course, that's just the crude version of the theory: it only explains how you talk about things you can actually see. But since language works through metaphors, as many scholars argue, you can use concrete images to talk about abstract concepts as well.

> But since language works through metaphors, as many scholars argue, you can use concrete images to talk about abstract concepts as well.

The anatomy of an animal's brain mirrors the way the animal gets information about its surroundings. Llamas make a living grazing, so the area of llama brain devoted to lip sensation is bigger than the combined areas devoted to sensations from all the rest of its body. Bats avoid obstacles by bouncing sound off their surroundings and listening to the echoes; accordingly, they have a huge auditory cortex.

Stored in Sereno's lab in the Cognitive Sciences Building are drawer after drawer of thin-sectioned animal brains, from rats to ground squirrels to various species of monkey. Each translucent slice of brain is affixed to a slide and carefully labeled; each of them, Sereno says, illustrates one more event in the expansion of the visual cortex.

He began accumulating slides as a student in Chicago, and he has continued doing so ever since. He is especially interested in defining the boundaries of primate visual areas. Though researchers claimed there were as many as 25, the borders of all but a few were too subtle to be detected without electrophysiological mapping. "In a way the work was tedious," he says, "like being an anatomist in 1600 and discovering where the bones are."

The experiments themselves are painstaking. First the animal is anesthetized, and a small hole is opened in its skull. A tiny electrode, finer than a hair, is implanted in the animal's brain, and its eyes are trained on a half-sphere of clear plastic marked with a grid. Then a light source is passed behind the plastic; when the implanted electrode picks up the signal of a neuron firing, the researchers know that the site of the electrode marks the portion of visual cortex that processes that precise point in the animal's visual field. Then the electrode is moved and the process is repeated. A single experiment routinely establishes up to 600 such points and may run up to 90 hours.

To the untutored eye, each of the thousands of slides Sereno and his students have generated over the years is an amorphous gray blob, devoid of anatomy. To Sereno, though, every one is rich with information. "See the whiskers?" he says, pointing at an area of a thin section with the tip of a pencil. Sure enough, a couple of dozen tiny white dots cluster in the sensory area of the rat brain, each marking the spot in the cortex where the sensation from a single whisker is processed.

Sereno puts the slide of a ground squirrel, a rodent not much bigger than a rat, on the light table. Because the squirrel uses vision instead of touch to find its way around, its whisker areas are actually somewhat smaller than the rat's. Its primary visual area, however, is four times bigger. And the higher-level visual areas have expanded even more. "Look—this is a *giganto* visual area," Sereno says, pointing to a place in the squirrel brain called TP. "It's eight times bigger than the equivalent rat area." Overall, the squirrel's brain is two to three times the size of the rat's, mostly because it has so much more volume devoted to vision. "This is my model for how our brains expanded," Sereno explains.

It's not, however, the model that has informed most notions about the brain since the Middle Ages. Medieval scholars figured there had to be some central place in the human brain where the straw of raw sensory input got turned into the gold of thought; where the visual image of a steeple and the sound of a bell combined to create the idea of "church." These philosophers called the hypothetical area the common sensorium, from which we get our term *common sense.* The idea that this common sensorium existed, and was the sole property of humans, persisted for centuries. But as nineteenth-century and early-twentieth-century researchers began to map the brains of animals, from rats to higher primates, they found no such area. What they did find was that much of the cortex was committed to so-called lower functions—sensory input and motor function.

Nevertheless, the idea of the common sensorium remained influential in the budding science of neuropsychology; researchers were convinced that human brains had to be different. After all, monkeys are smarter than lemurs, apes are smarter than monkeys, and we're smarter than apes. Perhaps as one went up the evolution-ary ladder, scientists thought, the area of the brain devoted to com-bining and analyzing raw sensory input—no longer called the common sensorium but the polymodal cortex—would get bigger and bigger. It seemed logical to think our smarts came from all that polymodal cortex just sitting there under our skulls, waiting to think.

Logical perhaps, but probably wrong, "Cognition seems so uni-fied, somehow," agrees Sereno. "It makes sense that there should be a place in there where everything comes together and the mind works on it. But from what we see, it doesn't look like the brain is wired that way." On the contrary, as the cortex has expanded, the increase has been in areas devoted to one modality or another. "To me," Sereno says, "this suggests that much of the computation done by the cortex"—functions such as language and thought—"is tied to one or another modality." He believes we use our visual areas as our primary means of processing language because they're what we use to make sense of our surroundings. "If you were a talking bat, you would process language with your auditory system. If you were a platypus, you'd use the cortical areas dedicated to your bill."

Until recently, there were virtually no data on exactly how the human cortex was parceled out, because noninvasive technology to investigate localization of brain function hadn't been invented yet. Since most people are understandably reluctant to have electrodes poked into their brains in the interest of science, data had to come from patients who had suffered injuries in particular regions of the brain.

The last five years, however, have seen an explosion in brain-imaging technology, an explosion to which Sereno and his colleagues have made profound contributions. Discovering what parts of our brains we use for what kinds of thought requires imaging techniques that provide instantaneous, well-localized signals of brain activity. Until around 1990, the available technology—electroencephalography, or EEG, and magnetoencephalography, or MEG—was inadequate for the task. These techniques record the brain's electrical impulses as fast as they happen but don't reveal where they originate.

In the early nineties Sereno and then–graduate student Anders Dale figured out how to make a computer combine the data from MEG and EEG and determine where the signals were coming from. They still needed a surface on which to display their findings, so Dale wrote the first computer program that could automatically reconstruct a three-dimensional picture of the brain from a set of two-dimensional magnetic resonance images, or MRIs. As a bonus, this program can plump up the resulting image of the highly fissured brain like a raisin in a steamer; on the gently inflated cortex, the boundaries of each cortical area can be precisely traced. This tech-

> ... fMRI can reveal which areas of the brain are working on particular tasks; it thus provides a localized picture of ongoing brain activity ...

nique turned out to be of enormous benefit to researchers trying to draw the boundaries of what Sereno calls "states in the cortical country."

Sereno and his collaborators have recently set out to map human visual areas using a noninvasive technique called functional magnetic resonance imaging, or fMRI. By using magnetic fields to measure changes in blood flow to the brain, fMRI can reveal which areas of the brain are working on particular tasks; it thus provides a localized picture of ongoing brain activity (though it doesn't catch split-second changes, the way EEG and MEG can). At last, with the technology to record brain activity in real time, and a smooth, unfolded surface on which to display it, Sereno has all the tools at his disposal to prove, or fail to prove, his vision-language theory.

Over the past few years Sereno and his wife, Claudia (a social worker with San Diego's homeless), along with neurobiologist Roger Tootell of the Massachusetts General Hospital Nuclear Magnetic Resonance Center in Boston, some friends, colleagues, and a few paid volunteers, have entombed themselves for hours at a stretch in an fMRI scanner. While the subject lies motionless, Sereno or an assistant flashes images—sometimes patterns, sometimes words—on a screen a few inches away.

In its own way, this work is as hard on the researchers as the marathon neurophysiology experiments. The subjects, supine on a table, are slid into a huge metal tube nearly ten feet long and six feet in diameter. They clench a bite bar between their jaws to keep their heads steady and must focus their eyes intently, since even a very small eye motion muddies the results. They wear metal cages on their heads for mapping, and earplugs to block the 100-decibel clanking of the giant magnet. "I think it's sort of cozy, myself," says Sereno. "It's kind of a Zen thing. Of course, you have to remember not to drink too much coffee."

Through this scanner work, Sereno has discovered that linguistic tasks produce a high level of activity in areas of his subjects' brains that, had those friends and colleagues been monkeys, would be higher visual areas. What's more, the levels of activity are much higher in those areas when the subjects are shown meaningful sentences than when they're shown random words. Other researchers, he adds, have found that stimulating those areas with electrodes inhibits speech production in much the same way that stimulating the "classical" language areas of Broca and Wernicke does.

As support for his theory, these results aren't much yet, but they're a start. "I'd say the onus is on people to show clearly there's some evidence of a new language area that just got stuck in there," says Sereno. "The default position is to assume that the human brain is more or less like animal brains, but we use it in different ways."

Several years ago, Sereno recalls, he was giving a talk at Ohio State, a stronghold of ape cognition research. He broached one of his favorite analogies: the one between birdsong and human language. "Some guy got up and said, 'Are you trying to tell me you think birds have more sophisticated vocal learning than apes?' And I said, 'Well, yes. Absolutely.'

"The main thing you notice about nonhuman primates and vocal learning is how bad they are at it," he explains. "Songbirds are easily a thousand times better."

Two of the most important properties of language, Sereno points out, are syntax, which is roughly equivalent to structure, and semantics, which is roughly equivalent to meaning. The natural communication system of apes has semantics aplenty, he says, but no syntax; ape calls can be put together in any order without changing the meaning. Further, most nonhuman primate communication is limbic—emotionally determined—rather than learned. A monkey deaf from birth will make the full range of monkey calls; a deafened songbird chick, on the other hand, will not sing.

The learning ability of songbirds is what makes Sereno think that comparing birdsong with human speech might be productive. Chicks spend several months listening to mature birds singing before they begin to imitate. Then they produce "subsong," meaningless sounds analogous to human baby babbling. A little later they start to produce fragments of songs. Finally they produce adult songs, sometimes hundreds of distinct ones, each comprising up to 20 song fragments, or syllables, concatenated.

> The learning ability of songbirds is what makes Sereno think that comparing birdsong with human speech might be productive.

In Sereno's view, then, birds have all the prerequisites for language: they have the vocal machinery, they have the distinct sounds, they have the capacity to string sounds together. The only thing they lack is semantics. "If birds had anything to say," he says, "they could definitely say it. But evidently they don't, because most birdsong is just a bizarrely elaborated way of saying 'Get out of here!' or 'Mate with me!'"

In the Sereno version of human language evolution, hominids might have developed the capacity to make noises like birdsong—sounds without much semantic content. They could have done it to attract mates, he thinks, an idea not without precedent. After all, some birdsong experts think the phenomenon of elaborate song arose because it signaled reproductive fitness, and that the bird with the capacity for the greatest amount of sustained song is the fittest mate.

If true, this scenario gets language evolution over its big hurdle: the time frame. Many anthropologists believe that humans began to speak somewhere toward the end of the last 100,000 years. For evidence they point to the sudden appearance of many new types of stone tools—a phenomenon Sereno calls "this incredible riffing in stone"—after nearly a million years of little change. Some take this to mean that humans were finally able to think symbolically, to remember complicated sequences, to communicate instructions.

But the question is, how? Making language in the human sense is not merely a complicated mental problem but a complicated anatomic problem as well. Take, for instance, the position of the larynx, the opening from the windpipe that connects the lungs with the throat. It is high up in the throat of nonhuman primates, so the root of the tongue can shield the opening during eating and drinking.

Technical details like larnyx placement have caused many scenarios for the evolution of language to come apart.

Humans are born with a high larynx. By the time we start to talk, however, the larynx has descended to a low position. Some researchers think our low larynx is what enables us to speak intelligibly: the tongue has room to move around and form vowels without blocking the larynx. This placement has a major disadvantage, though, putting us at risk of choking every time we eat or drink.

Technical details like larynx placement have caused many scenarios for the evolution of language to come apart: Why would natural selection have exposed humans to anatomic risks unless language was developed enough to provide an important survival advantage? But how could language have developed enough to provide an important selective advantage if no one had the vocal equipment to speak it?

The birdsong analogy solves the problem. If the pressure of sexual selection, not the pressure to communicate, was driving the refinement of the vocal machinery, that process could have been going on throughout hominid evolution. Then, when Sereno's proposed "relatively minor" neural rewiring of the visual system made language possible, the vocal mechanism could already have been up and running, waiting to pronounce the first meaningful words.

What if, Sereno suggests in an as yet unpublished paper, early humans had evolved "an elaborate system of essentially phonetic vocalizations, a kind of 'talking song' with no component semantics?" And he adds, in a burst of lyricism, "Perhaps early hominid pairs dueted like bay wrens, virtually innocent of reference."

To date, Sereno's idea about the connection between vision and language has circulated mostly among his immediate circle of colleagues. True, he's floated the theory at a few meetings and seminars, and he's published abbreviated treatments in journals specializing in knotty philosophical-scientific problems, such as the *Journal of Theoretical Biology*. But he's never given the vision-into-language theory a full-length, full-fledged airing in a peer-reviewed journal. This is largely because the sort of hard evidence that might convince literal-minded colleagues—fMRI scans, for instance, rather than compelling analogies—is only beginning to come in. ("But now that I've got tenure," Sereno says, laughing and rubbing his hands together in exaggerated anticipation, "I'm really going to hit this hard.")

While few neuroscientists are prepared to go all the way to presemantic, prelapsarian duetting hominids with Sereno, the skepticism with which they tend to regard the idea is tempered by their respect for his more mainstream work. Linguists, on the other hand, are cutting Sereno a little less slack. But the skeptical reactions of colleagues seem to energize Sereno rather than discourage him. "I know," he says cheerfully, "I'm really extreme. A lot of times, progress happens when somebody is slightly nervous in another field. It's scary when you start out—like when you go into a seminar room and you don't even understand the words people are using. But I think you're more flexible, more attentive, less hidebound when you're afraid someone may call you a dilettante."

Why Andy Couldn't Read

By Pat Wingert and Barbara Kantrowitz

A ndrew Mertz was a very unhappy little boy in 1995. Third grade was a disaster, the culmination of a crisis that had been building since he entered kindergarten in suburban Maryland. He couldn't learn to read, and he hated school. "He would throw temper tantrums in the morning because he didn't want to go," recalls his mother, Suzanne. The year before, with much prodding from Suzanne, the school had authorized diagnostic tests for Andrew. The results revealed a host of brain processing problems that explained why he kept mixing up letters and sounds. Andrew's problem now had a label—he was officially classified as learning disabled—and he was legally entitled to help. But school officials, claiming bureaucratic delays, didn't provide any extra services.

In desperation, Suzanne, a trained reading specialist, pulled Andrew out of school and taught him at home for 10 months. It was an awesome task. To Andrew, lowercase p, q, b and d all looked like sticks with circles attached. Suzanne taught through touch and sound. She spent hours helping him make letters out of Play-Doh, shaving cream, sand and rice while exaggerating the sounds that went with them. The next year the district agreed to place him in a high-quality program for "gifted" children with learning disabilities. Teachers there continued many of the same practices. Now, at 10, Andrew is still struggling, but at least he can finally read.

Just about every teacher knows students like Andrew Mertz, bright kids who can't learn—no matter how hard they try. They are a painful puzzle to their parents and the subject of an intense educational controversy. In the last few years, researchers have made great strides in identifying and treating learning problems. But the explosion in knowledge has also led to what some say is an epidemic of diagnoses. According to 1996 figures, 2.6 million kids (4.36 percent of the nation's students) were in publicly funded learning-disabilities programs. In 1977, about 800,000 (1.8 percent of the student body) had been diagnosed. And this may only be the beginning. In an astonishing estimate, some researchers now say that as many as 20 percent of schoolchildren may have a neurological deficit, ranging from mild to severe, that makes it hard for them to read and write.

> Learning disorders are often hard to accept because they afflict kids who appear perfectly healthy.

That's a lot of kids—and trying to help them is expensive. Largely as a result of lobbying by parents, federal law now mandates a "free and appropriate education" for the learning disabled; districts even have to pay tuition at private schools if they can't provide appropriate services. Teachers and clinicians have devised a wide range of techniques— from having kids write letters in sandboxes to using tape recorders, computers and other special equipment—to combat specific disabilities. The price tag: $8.12 billion last year, according to the Center for Special Education Finance.

This revolution has bred a new wave of critics who sneer at the learning-disabilities "epidemic." Some say many students labeled learning disabled are just lazy and looking for an easy way out. Other critics blame bad teaching for kids' reading problems and claim that school officials are inflating the number of disabled kids in order to wrest more money from the government. Still others contend that overly pushy parents—stereotypical hyperambitious Yuppie strivers—are behind the dramatic increase in the numbers of learning-disabled students. These parents, the critics say, need a scientific excuse to explain why Jason or Jennifer isn't Harvard med-school material. The skeptics include prominent educators, like Boston University president Jon Westling, who was sued by students after he clamped down on accommodations for learning-disabled students.

But to parents whose children are struggling in school, the "epidemic" is real and heartbreaking. Learning disorders are often hard to accept because they afflict kids who appear perfectly healthy. It's easy to grasp the problems encountered by a child with a physical incapacity, such as blindness or paralysis. Yale University pediatrician and neuroscientist Sally Shaywitz, who studies the complex of reading problems called dyslexia, says a learning problem is a "hidden disability." In fact, learning-disabled kids often display talent in other areas—perhaps art or science—while failing in one or more of the three R's.

Tammy Hollingsworth of suburban Dallas was optimistic when Joey, the oldest of her four children, entered kindergarten 15 years age. Teachers had told her the boy was a genius. "His IQ was over 150 and he had a photographic memory," she recalls. But as he grew older and schoolwork became harder, he ran into serious problems. "Any assignment that required a transfer from the brain to paper, forget it. He couldn't do it." Over the years, teachers told Hollingsworth that Joey was just lazy and a discipline problem.

> **Any assignment that required a transfer from the brain to paper, forget it. He couldn't do it.**

He was 15 years old before he was tested for learning disabilities. Although the results showed he had real problems expressing his thoughts in writing (a disorder technically known as dysgraphia), it was too late to save his school career. Years of frustration and failure had taken their toll, and he dropped out at 17. Joey eventually earned a high-school-equivalency diploma; he is now enrolled in a local police academy.

If Joey were entering kindergarten today, he might have a better chance. The term "learning disabilities" is relatively new. It was introduced in 1963, when parents and educators from around the country organized the nonprofit group now known as the Learning Disabilities Association. Until then, children with learning problems were generally classified as "perceptually handicapped," "brain injured" or "neurologically impaired." Many were turned away from public schools as uneducable, and if they couldn't afford private-school tuition, they just stayed home; some were even labeled mentally retarded. One advantage of combining the old diagnoses under a single new term was that it enabled educators to distinguish between children with below-average IQs (who were then put into classes for the mentally retarded) and kids of average or above-average intelligence who had trouble learning in specific areas but otherwise functioned normally.

More than three decades later, there is still no universal agreement about how to classify the constellation of problems that fall under this umbrella diagnosis. Medical doctors tend to accentuate differences in genetics, as well as brain organization and function.

Psychologists focus on dysfunctions in areas like perception, processing, memory and attention. Teachers zero in on the specific areas of academic difficulty.

But researchers are getting closer to some concrete answers. The most tantalizing clues are coming from brain research that is still in the early stages, which is very promising. Using state-of-the-art functional magnetic resonance imaging (fMRI)—machines that take pictures of the brain in action—scientists are investigating disruptions in specific neurosystems. And they're learning even more from examining children and adults with brain injuries, says Martha Bridge Denckla, a neuropsychologist with the Kennedy Krieger Institute in Baltimore. "Some of these traumatic brain cases simulate the exact picture we see all the time in learning-disabled cases where we don't know the cause," Denckla says.

> **The most common learning disabilities relate to language—reading, writing and spelling.**

"These experiences make me very confident that what is causing LD affects the brain." But there's a long way to go. It was only four years ago that Shaywitz's team took one of the first fMRI pictures of a brain caught in the act of reading.

This is the most critical area of research because the most common learning disabilities relate to language—reading, writing and spelling. Some children have trouble comprehending words or letters in sequence. Others read words but don't understand the content. Still others are dyslexics, children and adults who have trouble naming letters and sounding out words, despite the fact that they often have large vocabularies and reason well.

Because dyslexia seems to run in families, scientists think that it is often inherited. For years, researchers suspected it was caused by vision problems, and a stereotype developed that dyslexics commonly reverse letters (reading d's as b's, for example). Today, researchers like Yale's Shaywitz say dyslexics are no more likely to reverse letters than anyone else. Instead, Shaywitz and other researchers theorize that dyslexia is linked to a glitch in the brain's wiring that interferes with the ability to translate a written word into units of sound, or phonemes. Scientists have found that dyslexics often cannot recognize and break down spoken words into their phonetic segments or slice off one phoneme from a word—for example, they cannot figure out that "bat" without the b is "at."

Technically, this problem is known as a "phonological awareness" deficit.

Researchers have identified four distinct steps in learning to read; breakdowns anywhere in this process can explain severe reading problems. G. Reid Lyon, acting chief of the child-development and behavior branch of the National Institutes of Child and Human Development, says that reading for all children begins with phonological awareness. Combinations of just 44 phonemes produce every English word. "Children who will be good readers," Lyon says, "just have a knack for understanding that words are made up of different sounds before they learn anything about the alphabet." The next step is linking these sounds with specific letters. This can be confusing because most letters—in English and many other languages—can have more than one sound. The reading-instruction methods known as linguistics (sound to letters) and phonics (letters to sound) focus on this part of the process by having kids sound out words. The third step, Lyon says, is for a child to become a fast reader—to make the association between symbol and sound virtually automatic so that the child can move on to the final step, concentrating on the meaning of the words. (Researchers around the country are testing ways to put these findings into reading programs for all kids, not just learning-disabled children.)

> **Scientists have found that dyslexics often cannot recognize and break down spoken words into their phonetic segments . . .**

Some children also have spoken-language problems, which are often ignored because parents are told kids will "grow out of it." Kids with this disorder might mispronounce words because they're not processing sounds correctly. For example, they might call animals "aminals." They may also confuse specific sounds (thumb could become "fum") well after their peers are speaking clearly. School is a frustrating experience because they can't demonstrate what they know. They may, for example, recognize colors but not be able to name them. And their school troubles don't stop there. Studies indicate that preschoolers with oral-language problems often have difficulty later learning to read and write.

Another group of learning disorders revolves around difficulties in learning to compute or reason mathematically. In severe cases, these problems are called dyscalculia. Sometimes math difficulties appear without any other learning problems. At other times, these are the same children who have difficulty learning to speak and read. Janet Lerner, professor of education at Northeastern Illinois University and the author of the classic textbook for teachers of learning-disabled children, says some kids with math disabilities may suffer from "visual motor" problems that may make it difficult for them to count objects without physically touching them. They also have trouble adding one group of objects to another without counting them out, one by one. Others may have "visual perception" problems that, for example, render them unable to see a triangle as anything but three unrelated lines. They find it very arduous to copy letters and numbers and align numbers properly for computation.

> ... many learning-disabled children also have a variety of motor, social, memory, organizational and attention problems that affect their schoolwork ...

Complicating the picture is the fact that many learning-disabled children also have a variety of motor, social, memory, organizational and attention problems that affect their schoolwork, such as attention deficit disorder (ADD). Researchers estimate that up to 30 percent of children with learning disabilities may have ADD, which makes it even harder for them to focus. Children humiliated by their inability to overcome their learning problems also tend to develop behavioral and emotional disorders. Kids with learning problems are twice as likely to drop out of school; a disturbingly high number end up with criminal records.

Even after they learn to read, write and add, many learning-disabled people don't find these basic skills easy. That's why educators believe early intervention is critical. "If we do not identify children early, by the end of second grade, the majority of them will have difficulty reading for the rest of their lives," says Lyon. "What we're finding is that there are sensitive periods when children can learn to read more easily, just like there are windows when children learn foreign language easier."

In many clinics and hospitals around the country, such as Evanston Northwestern Healthcare's Evanston Hospital north of Chicago, babies and toddlers who had a traumatic birth are regularly checked for signs of developmental delays—significant lags in reaching the milestones of smiling, sitting, walking and talking. "We know problems at birth, including prematurity, increase the chances of developing learning problems later in childhood," says Joanne

Bregman, director of Evanston's child-development clinic. "All the research says that the first three years of life are critical. The sooner a problem is identified, the sooner it can be treated and the better the outcome is likely to be." Early intervention usually consists of speech, occupational or physical therapy. Every state has outreach programs that funnel children exhibiting significant delays in development into specialized public preschools.

A few nursery schools formally screen all children for early signs of learning problems. In Washington, D.C., Lynn A. Balzer-Martin, a pediatric occupational therapist, begins her multipart screening with a thorough questionnaire to parents and teachers about a child's health history, behavior and activities. Then she observes the child's movements, taking note of balance, positioning and coordination. Brain research has shown that the way a child moves or follows instruction can be an indicator of how well he processes information.

> . . . the way a child moves or follows instruction can be an indicator of how well he processes information.

Someday, intervention may begin even earlier. Geneticists are working on procedures to identify inherited learning disorders. John DeFries, director of the Institute of Behavioral Genetics at the University of Colorado, says that researchers now believe that although as many as 20 genes may be involved in the reading process, just two or three "may account for most of the variation in reading difficulty that we see." If scientists can identify these genes, they could someday screen kids to determine which are at risk, and start working with them before they start to flounder.

At the moment, early intervention and diagnosis is the exception rather than the rule. Most children with learning disabilities don't get help until they're well along in school—usually between the ages of 9 and 14. That's because, under the law, funding follows failure. Children who are officially labeled learning disabled are eligible for special aid. But to win that, all 50 states and the federal government require proof of school problems.

Of course, that doesn't mean every child who is having trouble in school is learning disabled. Most states require a discrepancy between a child's actual achievement levels and his intellectual potential, usually determined by some type of IQ test. And that's another reason learning disabilities have become so controversial.

Many critics of IQ tests believe they are culturally biased and under-estimate the intellectual potential of poor and minority children. "Black kids have to be more severely disabled to be called LD," says Esther Minskoff of James Madison University. "White kids are picked up earlier."

Public and private schools around the country have developed programs for learning-disabled kids; the quality varies widely. At the Lab School of Washington, a private school with 285 students in kindergarten through 12th grade, founder and director Sally Smith uses the arts—especially music, dance, painting, drama and filmmaking—to teach academic skills. She has also created clubs based on different time periods to help develop social skills as well as provide a lively history curriculum. Kids start out as cavemen and move through Egypt, the Middle Ages and the Renaissance up to modern times. "It's very experiential, very hands-on," Smith says. "We want to build on their strengths." (One of the authors of this article, Washington correspondent Pat Wingert, sends a child to the Lab School.)

Public-school programs generally have fewer resources, but teachers still try to emphasize individual attention. At Eagle Rock Elementary School in suburban Los Angeles, Joyce Jerome and two aides preside over a class of 14 learning-disabled students in grades four to six. This year's theme is the ocean, and Jerome has decorated a wall with fishing nets, colorful seashells and pictures of whales and other sea life.

One recent morning, five students—all of whom read well below their grade level—were gathered around a half-moon desk trying to read the word "enormous." Finally, one child blurted out "eee nor moose" and smiled. He won a "ticket," which can be redeemed for prizes like colored pencils and carnival-type toys in the classroom "store."

Another student, an 11-year-old girl, gets the word "nothing." She is told to break it into syllables and does so after some obvious stress. Finally, she says two words: "no thing." Jerome prompts her. "What is like no thing? What sounds like no thing?" The girl rubs her forehead with her palm. "I don't know," she says, exasperated. "Why are these words so complicated?"

Some critics of the idea of learning disabilities claim that better instruction could eliminate the problem altogether. In the last few years, much of the controversy over these problems has become entwined with the often ferocious dispute over two alternate methods of teaching reading: phonics and "whole language," which is based on children's grasping the meaning of a word from its context in a story. While a pure whole-language approach works well for some kids, others—especially those with learning disabilities—struggle to read without help in phonics.

A few researchers have even suggested that whole language is the main reason for the huge increase in the number of kids diagnosed as disabled—fueling the idea that learning disabilities is a phony diagnosis, perhaps contrived to compensate for what are really teaching disabilities. In her new book, "Why Our Children Can't Read," Diane McGuinness, a Florida psychologist, maintains that all children need direct instruction in decoding words and that the proportion of children labeled learning disabled would drop if whole-language programs were replaced with those that emphasize phonological awareness and linguistics.

> If a family can't work through the bureaucratic maze, a child can languish.

Learning disabilities are hard to understand, and so is the law that attempts to help struggling kids. If a family can't work through the bureaucratic maze, a child can languish. Such was the case with Jennie Harvey. At 15, she's finally learning to read at the Cove School in suburban Chicago. Because she had severe speech problems, Jennie was enrolled in special-ed classes at the age of 3. Although she was promoted annually, by the seventh grade she still wasn't reading at a first-grade level. Her parents accepted Jennie's teachers' assessment that they were doing all they could. But three years ago they hired Rose Pech, a retired special-education teacher turned tutor, who diagnosed a series of problems that required much more specialized instruction than Jennie had been receiving. With Pech's help, Jennie was admitted to Cove, a private school for severely learning-disabled children (the state pays the $16,000 annual tuition because the district cannot provide the same services). Jennie's story is an extreme example of lost potential; because she's learning to read so late, her teachers doubt that she can ever really catch up.

Scientists want to spare other children a similar fate. And parents like Suzanne Mertz are learning how to make the system work for their kids. When her husband was recently transferred to Pennsylvania, she went school-shopping for Andrew before deciding which town to live in. She finally settled on Great Valley, which has an excellent learning-disabilities program. Her advice to other parents? "You can advocate for your child better than anyone," she says. "You know them best." Raising a child with learning disabilities will always be a long, hard road—but now, at least, there's reason to hope.

A Head for Numbers

by Robert Kunzig

Everybody has one—even rats and pigeons, to say nothing of people. The ability to grasp small numbers and map them into a "number line" in the brain is an evolutionary birthright of ours. Arithmetic, of course, is another matter.

Nobody knew precisely what had happened to Monsieur N.; perhaps he had just tripped, or maybe it was a stroke that had triggered the fall and the consequent blow to his head. He showed up at a hospital in Orléans one day in 1986 with a giant hematoma in his brain's left hemisphere. The surgeons kept him from bleeding to death, but they couldn't keep the lesion from growing even larger as they worked. By the time they were done, large parts of his left temporal, parietal, and occipital lobes—the rear half of the hemisphere, essentially—were useless. By the time Stanislas Dehaene came to see him, three years later, it was clear that N. was going to be severely impaired for life. It was a sad business: the man was in his early 40s, had been a successful salesman, was married with two young daughters—only now his wife and kids had left him and he had been forced to move back in with his aging parents. Dehaene, a young neuropsychologist with a family of his own, felt the burden of sympathy as much as anyone would. But he also felt something else, and seven years later his face still brightens at the recollection. The first question he asked N. was "What's 2 plus 2?" When N. answered "3," Dehaene knew he had landed a spectacular case.

That encounter took place at the Hôpital de la Salpêtrière in Paris, where Dehaene's friend and research partner, Laurent Cohen, works as a neurologist. N.'s provincial doctor had sent him to the well-known medical center to seek help from the specialists. There was in fact little to be done for him, and treating N. was not Dehaene's or Cohen's job anyway. Their interest was in finding out what the trauma had left of his ability to process numbers. And as they questioned him closely, what was left turned out to be far more substantial than his performance on 2 plus 2 would have indicated. Even his dramatic failure on tests like that one was suggestive. N. might say that 2 plus 2 was 3, or that it was 5, but never that it was 9 or 47. He was never absurd.

N. had lost the ability to calculate—but not, it seemed, to approximate. Numbers existed for him *only* as approximations, which became increasingly fuzzy the larger they got. It was not just his arithmetic that was affected; his memory for number facts was similarly blurred. A year had "about 350 days," a month "15 or 20." N. had no precise knowledge of the meaning of "9," but he knew that 9 children was "too much" for one mother and too few for a whole school. Dehaene asked him how many eggs in a *douzaine,* and he did not answer *douze,* the French word for 12; he said "6 or 10." "Six or 10," though, isn't "60 or a hundred." It is close to the mark. Somewhere deep within the posterior folds of his brain, N. still had an intuitive, almost primordial sense of numbers.

> Somewhere deep within the posterior folds of his brain, N. still had an intuitive, almost primordial sense of numbers.

This was of course little consolation to him. When N. realized that he could not tell whether a number was odd or even, and was just guessing, he became so upset that Dehaene had to stop the experiment.

In the January 15, 1880, issue of the journal *Nature,* the British anthropologist Francis Galton published a curious little research note of the kind you could still publish a century ago. As part of a general study of mental imagery, Galton had passed around a questionnaire to a bunch of friends and acquaintances, asking them to report on whether they could "see" numbers and if so in what way. Some of them could, it seemed, mostly the women. ("I have been astonished to find how superior women usually are to men in the vividness of their mental imagery and their powers of introspection. . . ." Galton wrote. "The former usually show an unexpected amount of intelligence, while many of the latter are as unexpectedly obtuse.")

Usually the numbers were arranged along a line, or a series of lines, that got progressively less distinct and sometimes vanished into the mental distance as the numbers got larger. Sometimes the numbers had color or texture ("There are sorts of woolly lumps at the tens," one subject reported). And on occasion they had a great deal of personality: "9 is a wonderful being of whom I felt almost afraid, 8 I took for his wife . . . 6, of no particular sex but gentle and straightforward. . . ." That report came from an unusually visual male philosopher.

Galton himself considered his results a curiosity—interesting mainly for the extent to which they showed the tendency of mental traits to run in families. (He was an early eugenicist.) Not until 1967 did another paper in *Nature* provide evidence that all of us have a mental number line of sorts, even those 95 percent of us, according to the available evidence, who cannot see it. Two Stanford psychologists, Robert Moyer and Thomas Landauer, measured the time it took a person to choose the larger of two single typed digits by flipping either a left-hand or right-hand switch. They found that it took at least half a second. But the smaller the difference between the two numbers, the longer it took: deciding between 6 and 7, say, took more than a tenth of a second longer than deciding between 1 and 9. This "distance effect" suggested strongly that the brain was converting the digits into analog magnitudes—line segments, for instance—before comparing them. Choosing between two lines is obviously harder the closer in length they are.

> . . . all of us have a mental number of sorts, even those 95 percent of us . . . who cannot see it.

Since then the distance effect has been verified again and again, notably by Stanislas Dehaene. Dehaene did his Ph.D. dissertation on it, at the Ecole des Hautes Etudes en Sciences Sociales in Paris, where he continued to do research until the end of last year. (He now heads a team of researchers at INSERM, the French equivalent of the National Institutes of Health, outside Paris in Orsay.) It was while doing his doctoral work that he met Cohen, who was a graduate student in the same laboratory at the time. And it was not long after Dehaene finished his Ph.D. that he and Cohen met N. Monsieur N.—"the approximate man," Dehaene calls him—lent new significance to the number line. He clearly still had it—he could still tell which of two numbers was bigger, even though he could not readily read them aloud, let alone add or multiply them. Monsieur N. showed that the ability to grasp the meaning of numbers, by translating them into an approximate analog representation of quantity, and the ability to calculate precisely were two different processes occurring at least in part in different regions of the brain.

In a series of papers with Cohen, and most recently in a book published in France last January and due out this fall in the United States (English title: *The Number Sense*), Dehaene has sketched a rough model of how the brain processes numbers and does simple arithmetic. The core evidence for the model comes from brain-lesion patients. N.'s lesion was so large that he didn't reveal much about where the number line might be localized—except that it probably must be present in the right hemisphere as well as the left, since so much of his left hemisphere has been wiped out. But N. was hardly the first person, or the last, to suffer from "acalculia." As neurological deficits go, it is relatively common. In the 1920s and 1930s a Viennese neurologist named Josef Gerstmann had studied a series of such patients, and he had noted that they tended to have other deficits as well: they confused left and right; they couldn't name the fingers of the hand or find a finger when it was named for them ("finger agnosia"); and they couldn't write ("agraphia"). Gerstmann also noted that his patients all tended to have a lesion in one particular place: in the inferior parietal cortex of the left hemisphere—on the side of the brain, above and behind the ear.

"There are regions of the brain for which you can say in two words what they do," says Cohen. "The visual cortex—well, that's where visual information arrives. The primary motor region, that's where motor commands leave from. But the inferior parietal cortex is involved in a lot of things. It receives inputs from all sorts of sensory modalities and from the frontal cortex. So it's difficult to say in two words what it does: it does a lot of things."

But one of those things is process numbers. Cohen and Dehaene recently had as a patient a man called M., a retired artist. During coronary bypass surgery he had apparently lost blood flow to his brain, and more specifically to the right parietal cortex. Gerstmann's syndrome usually results from damage to the left parietal lobe, but M. was left-handed, which presumably meant that his brain was the mirror image of the norm. In any case, he had the gamut of Gerstmann's symptoms. In particular, his number line was a mess.

M. couldn't divide single digits; he couldn't say what number fell between two others. "This was perhaps the most spectacular thing in this patient," Dehaene recalls. "We'd say, 'What's between 2 and 4?' and he'd say, 'I have no idea—maybe 7?' He was wrong 80 percent of the time. And the thing was, he understood the task very well. He could do it with days of the week, for instance— 'What's between Tuesday and Thursday?' He would have no problem with that. Or what's between *b* and *d* in the alphabet, or re and fa in the musical scale—no problem. But purely when it had to do with quantities, numerical quantities, then he was lost." Subtraction also baffled M. "The subtraction test was stopped," Dehaene and Cohen report, "after the patient failed on the tenth problem, which was 3 minus 1."

M.'s highly focal lesion—the rest of his brain was intact— localized the number line to the inferior parietal lobe. It said nothing, though, about how that part of the brain goes about representing numbers as quantities. "We know which area is involved, but we have absolutely no evidence of the neural code inside that area," says Dehaene. "My idea is that different neurons will be involved in coding different quantities. So if you are thinking of the quantity that is about 6, for instance, a certain population of neurons will light up. And *maybe* there is a topographical arrangement of these neurons on the cortical surface."

Maybe, in other words, the number line is not just a metaphor, as Dehaene sometimes says, for the brain's ability to represent numbers as analog quantities; maybe there is a literal number line hardwired into our brains, each number corresponding to a dedicated cluster of neurons, the clusters arranged one after another in the same order as the numbers themselves. It need not be that simple, but it could be: after all, vision works that way. An image falling onto the retina is mapped point-for-point onto neurons in the visual cortex without disrupting the image's geometry. And number, Dehaene thinks, is no different from the spatial relationships of objects in the visual field, or their color. It is one of the fundamental dimensions along which the brain constructs the world.

No one has yet studied the arithmetical abilities of brain-lesion patients who happen to be rats or pigeons or chimpanzees. And yet if you could and did, you might find something like the number line in them too. Rats can learn to press a lever 4 times or 16 times to get food, or to take the fourth left turn in a maze. Pigeons can learn to peck at a target 45 times rather than 50. Chimps will pick a tray with 7 chocolates over one with 6, although in number comparison they too suffer from the distance effect: when trying to choose the larger of two numbers, they are more likely to make a mistake if the two are close together. Chimps have even been taught to add fractions.

All this evidence, says Dehaene, shows that the elementary ability to perceive and manipulate number is part of our evolutionary heritage—something we're born with. Experiments with human babies bear this out. Perhaps the best known is the one reported a few years ago by Karen Wynn of the University of Arizona. Wynn displayed a Mickey Mouse doll to five-month-old infants, then hid it behind a screen; she then brought a second Mickey onstage in full view of the audience and shoved it behind the screen; then she dropped the screen. When she thereby revealed two Mickeys, the babies examined them for an average of around 13 seconds. But when, through a bit of experimental trickery, only one Mickey appeared behind the dropped screen, the babies stared an average of half a second longer, indicating that they were surprised at the vanished Mouse—and that they understood, Wynn says, that one plus one should equal two. A similar experiment showed they were also surprised by evidence that two minus one wasn't equal to one.

> ... the elementary ability to perceive and manipulate number is part of our evolutionary heritage—something we're born with.

Wynn, crossing both taxonomic and corporate boundaries, has since moved from Mickey Mouse to Daffy Duck: she has found that infants who have become accustomed to seeing a Daffy puppet execute three vertical jumps onstage, while furiously wagging its head between jumps in a distracting way, will be surprised if it jumps only twice, and vice versa. In other words, babies can count motions as well as objects—indicating, again, that they grasp the concept of number. Other experiments suggest they can count drumbeats. "Whatever mental process babies use to enumerate things, it's abstract," says Wynn. "It takes in 'units' at the most abstract level—which is what you need for an initial definition of number. If all your units are salt shakers, you haven't got number. But of all the kinds of things we've tested, babies can count them all."

Wynn's initial Mickey experiment has been reproduced by other researchers, including Dehaene. As he sees it, such experiments show that babies are born with a number line that allows them to grasp small quantities, up to three or perhaps four, and even to perform elementary arithmetic on them. As a baby grows into a child and eventually goes to school, two things happen. One is that the number line gets extended and refined as the child learns bigger numbers. The other is that the child learns to perform precise calculations that transcend what animals can do and what is possible with the number line. That is when other parts of the brain beside the inferior parietal lobe become involved. That is when number becomes linked to language.

Both brain hemispheres, in Dehaene and Cohen's model, can perceive Arabic digits. Both can extract meaning from those digits by locating them along the number line in the inferior parietal cortex. But only the language hemisphere—that is, the left hemisphere (except in some left-handers like M.) can calculate. The most direct evidence for this comes from patients in whom the link between hemispheres, the corpus callosum, has been severed by surgery or stroke. With split brains, as they're called, it is possible to present numbers or arithmetic problems to one hemisphere at a time, by displaying them in either the left or right visual field. In such experiments, the right hemisphere generally shows itself unable to pick the correct answer to elementary arithmetic problems. (The experiments do not require the subject to say the answer out loud; the right hemisphere would be inadequate to that task in any case.)

> But only the language hemisphere—that is, the left hemisphere (except in some left-handers like M.)—can calculate.

To do any arithmetic that transcends the crude capabilities of the number line, say Dehaene and Cohen, numbers have to be represented in the brain not only as digits but as words—because it is as words that the elementary facts of arithmetic are stored in memory. "That claim is very controversial," Dehaene says, particularly among non-French researchers. "I don't really understand why, but I wonder now whether there isn't some kind of cultural difference. Because in France it's really the way the facts are taught—at least multiplication, which is the paramount example. Maybe not so much now, but at least for the people we see as patients, they were trained, and I was trained, to recite multiplication facts—you know, the whole class together, 'Three times three: nine. Three times four:

twelve.' That's how you learn it. Maybe it is different in the States, and maybe it is different in the UK, where most of my colleagues are. They don't quite believe that verbal code is very important. But we have some fairly good evidence."

The evidence is called Madame B. She was a retired school-teacher, 60 years old when Dehaene and Cohen met her, with a lesion every bit as focal as M.'s but not in the inferior parietal lobe—she did not have

B. could still do subtraction because subtraction is not learned by rote.

Gerstmann's syndrome. Her lesion was not even in the cortex but near the center of the left hemisphere, in a multipart structure called the basal ganglia. Neural loops running between the cortex and the basal ganglia seem to be the repository for a lot of things we know so well we don't have to think about them—motor sequences like brushing our teeth, for instance, but also verbal sequences that have been drilled into our brains by rote memorization. B. had spent a career as drillmaster, inculcating class after class of young Stanislases and Laurents in the basics of French culture. Now, after her stroke, she could no longer recite the Lord's Prayer or the fables of La Fontaine; no longer sing "Au Clair de la Lune"; no longer say the alphabet even. And her multiplication tables were shattered.

"Perhaps I'm giving you the impression that she was very impaired," Dehaene goes on. "But in fact it was a very narrow domain of disability, because she could still read numbers, she could still write numbers, just like the other patients, and all the tasks that these patients could not do, she could do. On number comparisons she was all right, subtraction she was all right, absolutely no problem. There were all sorts of quantitative tasks she could do. 'What's between 2 and 4?'—she was perfect. So it was like a pure deficit of rote memory."

B. could still do subtraction because subtraction is not learned by rote. Subtraction involves other circuits in the language areas of the brain—Dehaene doesn't know which—and it is guided, as is division, by the quantitative intuition embodied in the number line. Multiplication and to a lesser extent addition are learned by rote—which is why M., with his number line gone from his verbal hemisphere but his basal ganglia intact, could still recite the multiplication table even while he failed to do 3 minus 1. His stroke had wiped out an intuition produced by millions of years of evolution, while sparing a veneer of education. In Madame B. the opposite had happened. M. had preserved the mechanics of arithmetic; she had preserved the meaning.

Stanislas Dehaene weathered the French system of mathematical education fairly well. From mastery of multiplication he went on, after high school, to pass the notoriously difficult mathematics exam that provides entry into the Ecole Normale Supérieure, one of France's elite schools. He had, as the French say, *la bosse des mathes*—literally, the bump for math. (It's an expression left over from phrenology, and it's also the title Dehaene chose for the French edition of his book—wryly, because the last thing he believes is that there is a single bump, a single center of arithmetic in the brain.) After getting his master's, though, Dehaene gave up doing mathematics in favor of trying to understand how the brain does it.

> I think it's better that children do the calculation with their calculators.

One conclusion he has reached after a decade of research is that the brain has a very hard time. "Rigorous calculations do not come easily to *Homo sapiens*," Dehaene writes in his book. "Like so many other animals, it is born with a fuzzy and approximate concept of number. . . . While our culture invented logic and arithmetic, our brain remained unchanged and restive even to the simplest algorithms." Dehaene believes that small *Homo sapiens,* of which he has three, should be spared this pain as much as possible. He believes they should be subjected to far less drilling in the multiplication tables and freed completely from the burden of long division, to say nothing of taking square roots by hand. He has no patience with the notion that such spadework builds character or even numerical intuition in children. He would hand them electronic calculators at the earliest possible age.

"The brain isn't capable of learning to do long division without concentrating on mechanics," he says. "It takes extreme concentration, and when you see the brain activity—it's enormous. It's really hard work. And meanwhile it's not concentrating on the meaning of what it's doing, and when it makes a mistake it's a monstrous one.

"I think it's better that children do the calculation with their calculators. At least then they have the result right away. They don't spend a minute thinking about how to get the result, and they can confront the size of the result with the number they started with and develop their intuition that way."

Some people have a prodigious arithmetical intuition that allows them to multiply or factor four-digit numbers in their heads, add much bigger ones at great speed, and in general skate up and down the number line with abandon. A few of these calculating prodigies have also been great mathematicians—Carl Friedrich Gauss, for example. Dehaene thinks prodigies and true mathematical geniuses are not so different from one another, and not so different, genetically, from the rest of us. Maybe their mental number lines are more vivid and detailed, as some of them have reported; certainly their memory for number facts must be far more expansive. Both those differences would have to be reflected somehow in the anatomy of their brains, but in Dehaene's view they are more likely to result from intense training at an early age than from an innate gift.

> "Do you really want to develop prodigies?" responds Dehaene.

"I'm talking about what you do to become an expert," he says. "If you ask people in the street, they'll tell you, 'Well, you know, it's done at birth. It's in your genes that you're a mathematician.' I don't believe that's how it is. I believe experts are people who work a tremendous amount, and if there is something in their genes, it's passion—the capacity to get excited about a tiny domain that's a bit abstract. Nowadays the only people who still become calculating prodigies are autistic people, because they're the only ones willing to concentrate on a domain that is after all very limited. The great mathematicians lose interest very rapidly. But the underlying mechanism is the same—it's that they're passionate. They work a tremendous amount, and in the end they develop an immense intimacy with mathematical objects." Wouldn't giving children electronic calculators discourage the development of precisely that sort of intimacy? "Do you really want to develop prodigies?" responds Dehaene.

No one really knows yet what a prodigy's or a mathematician's brain looks like. Dehaene is hoping to change that. The research center in Orsay is outfitted with the latest in brain-imaging equipment—PET and functional MRI scanners. Images of "normal" brains have already confirmed some of the findings from lesions—

that the inferior parietal cortex is active during most number processing, for instance, and that the left basal ganglia are especially active during multiplication. One day Dehaene would dearly like to run a few professional mathematicians through his MRI scanner while asking them to pick the larger of two numbers, multiply 8 by 7, and so on. It is possible he might find some area of the cortex that is systematically enlarged in the professionals.

Another study that both Dehaene and Cohen are excited about involves sticking hair-thin, needlelike electrodes into the brains of human subjects. This is not done to healthy people, of course. It is done to severe epileptics who are candidates for surgery: the electrodes are left in place for as long as a week, while the patient remains in the hospital, in the hopes of precisely locating the focal point of his seizures, the better to excise it. Dehaene and Cohen have hooked up with a team of surgeons at a hospital in Rennes who are allowing them to conduct number-processing experiments on willing patients during that week. The electrodes are so fine that they can record the electrical activity of small clusters of neurons. Sometimes an electrode may happen to be placed in the inferior parietal cortex. By examining many patients, Dehaene and Cohen think they have an outside chance of actually locating the number line. One day an electrode may penetrate a cluster of nerve cells that fire only when the patient sees, say, the number 6.

Another lucky breakthrough in their research would be to find another patient with a spectacular numerical disability. At the Salpêtrière, Cohen—part research neuropsychologist, part clinician in general neurology—spends most of his time treating people for sciatica and blurred vision and other run of the mill complaints. All the while he is hoping another Monsieur N. will walk through the door.

Cold January light is filtering through the window of the examination room, a yellow, antiseptic room devoid of personal detail or the slightest attempt at decor, where Cohen sits facing Madame F. across an old metal desk. She is fortyish, just a few years older than Cohen himself, but unlike Cohen, who is tieless, she is turned out for the exam. Bright red jacket, bottle-red hair, round red cheeks—one pictures her as a music hall actress rather than as the marketing manager she was until her recent disability. Having typecast her as a firecracker, one feels all the more the poignancy of her coming home from the hospital a month or so ago. One sees her looking helplessly at the washing machine and just not getting it—finally trying to read the directions, as if she hadn't already used the thing upwards of a thousand times. Or standing in the *métro*, the familiar *métro*, and staring at the route map, and just not getting it either; taking a friend along to be safe. Or going into her bank filled with anxiety because she couldn't be sure what number she would write on the check.

> One sees her looking helplessly at the washing machine and just not getting it . . .

When Cohen first examined Madame F., not long after a clot in her carotid artery had cut off the blood supply to two distinct areas of her left hemisphere—Broca's area, one of the language centers, and the inferior parietal cortex—she had serious problems with language, and she had especially serious problems with numbers. Cohen asked her to subtract 1 from 3: she couldn't do it. He asked her to read the time off his watch: she couldn't do it. He asked her to indicate what number should lie partway up a line labeled 0 at the bottom and 100 at the top—a schematic Celsius thermometer—and she said: "A million?" "She would just say anything at all," Cohen recalls. *"Anything at all."*

A month has gone by and Cohen is at last getting a chance to see her again; if he is to analyze her numerical deficit in detail, he will have to examine her many more times. "It's an enormous job to collect and interpret these data," he had explained before the session, "and in the end you get one article. So from time to time I have a patient like this, and I put in a lot of time and work, and then . . ." When you work as a cognitive neuropsychologist, there is always a tension between your interests as a scientist and your duties and emotions as a human—between wanting your subjects' brains to fail in a revealing way and wanting them to get better. Stroke victims very often get better, usually soon after the stroke. People with Gerstmann's syndrome, like Madame F., are especially known for it, for some reason. "There is a progressive improvement that takes place in the first days, weeks, and months—a spontaneous recuperation of part and sometimes of all the deficit," explains Cohen. "Often you see something interesting, and then . . ." When you're merely an observer watching a neuropsychologist examine a patient, you feel the same tension, with far less justification than the scientist himself.

"There is not much left here," Cohen finally says to Madame F., speaking of her disease, after she has read his watch a few times and raced through a series of arithmetic problems with only a few errors and normal hesitations: 3 plus 5, 5 plus 4, 13 minus 4, 12 minus 9, 6 divided by 2. It is not a special thing, this number sense that we share, in its elemental form, with rats and pigeons—no more special, to use Dehaene's analogy, than the ability to perceive space or color. Just the same, it is awful to be without it. Madame F. has lived through that, and today she is reduced to complaining to the doctor that her stroke has mysteriously banished her urge to smoke two packs of cigarettes a day. As Cohen pursues his battery of questions to completion, and Madame F. answers like an eager pupil—thoroughly unspectacular, thoroughly normal, thoroughly boring—it becomes clear that this woman will henceforth be lost to neuroscience. And that, all in all, it is better that way.

New Research on the Brain: Implications for Instruction

by Douglas Carnine

Gerald Edelman's work on the capacity of the human brain to categorize in connected ways has direct implications for educators, as Mr. Carnine makes clear.

T he dominant view of perception, recognition, memory, and learning originated with Plato: the brain is a block of wax; the world, a signet ring. This interpretation gained credence from a series of neurological discoveries, beginning in the late 19th century, which suggested that the brain consists of a collection of highly specialized functional regions. The doctrine of localization of function has strongly influenced many educators.

According to the currently modish learning styles movement, specific locations in the brain are associated with various functions—auditory, visual, tactile, and so forth—that are thought to be areas of "strength" or "weakness," depending on the individual. Once an individual's functional strengths have been identified, instructional methods that play to those strengths should be selected. With reading styles, for example, the language-experience approach emphasizes visual and tactile functions and so would be appropriate for a child with visual and tactile strengths.[1]

More recent research on the brain, by Gerald Edelman, Nobel laureate and director of the Neurosciences Institute at Rockefeller University, challenges such a simplified view of localization.[2] Israel Rosenfield describes Edelman's view of the brain:

What look like localizations are different ways of grouping stimuli—
parts of a process of creating possible appropriate combinations and
orderings of stimuli. . . . The "specialized centers" are just part of the
larger combinatory tactic (the procedures) of the brain.[3]

The central procedures in Edelman's scheme are categorization
and recategorization—in perception, in recognition, and in memory.
Rosenfield summarizes these three operations.

- "How we perceive stimuli depends on how they are catego-
rized, how they are organized in terms of other stimuli, not on their
absolute structure. . . ."[4]
- "Recognition of an object requires its categorization. And
categories are created by coupling, or correlating different samplings
of the stimuli." [5]
- "We do not simply store images or bits but become more
richly endowed with the capacity to categorize in connected ways." [6]

Categorization and recategorization might be viewed as the
overriding activities of the brain, serving as basic mechanisms for
various brain functions. A cornerstone of the capacity to categorize
is the learner's ability to note instances of sameness. The role that
noticing samenesses plays in learning has important implications for
instruction.

At first glance, categorization might appear to be a mundane
activity. After all, membership in a category obviously requires an
attribute of sameness: all vehicles share certain characteristics. However, noting samenesses can be far more creative than merely classifying objects as vehicles.

For example, near the turn of the century, a German physician
was vacationing in Egypt. He was asked to treat a severely stricken
boy who had been bitten by a cobra. When he inquired about the
incident, the physician found that the boy's father had been bitten
first but lacked the life-threatening symptoms present in his son. The
father said that he had been bitten on two previous occasions, with
the severity of the symptoms diminishing each time.

When he returned to Germany, the physician hypothesized that
the same thing might happen with diphtheria, which was ravaging
Europe at the time. He began a series of experiments in which he
injected horses with increasingly potent doses of diphtheria bacilli
until the horses developed antitoxins against the disease. Then he
developed a serum from the blood of the horses. The serum led to a
vaccine that immunized children against diphtheria.

Just as exposure to snake venom created immunity for the Egyptian boy's father, so injections of the diphtheria serum created immunity in European children. Today we have vaccines for polio, measles, and so forth. Immunization is a dramatic example of the importance of noting samenesses.

> The brain must try as many combinations of incoming stimuli as possible . . .

At the other extreme are cases in which we construe samenesses that are not only commonplace but also incorrect. Rosenfield notes that the mind is not a block of wax: learners are active as they categorize and recategorize. "But neither can one predict what constitutes information for an organism. The brain must try as many combinations of incoming stimuli as possible and then select those combinations that will help the organism relate to its environment."[7]

WHY MISTAKES MAKE SENSE

There is no way to "make" a learner focus on the combination of stimuli (i.e., note the samenesses) that the teacher wants to teach. Moreover, a student who learns an unintended sameness will make mistakes—perhaps trivial, perhaps significant. How students *mis*learn by noting unintended samenesses illustrates the educational relevance of this basic brain activity. Incidents of such mislearning begin in preschool and continue through the elementary and secondary grades.

Very young children know that the name of an object stays the same even after the orientation of the object has changed. For example, when a chair is turned to face the opposite direction, it remains a chair. Consequently, in preschool, when a *b* is flipped to face the opposite direction, children often assume that it still goes by the name of *b*. Making this error doesn't necessarily imply that a student's visual brain function is weak or that the student would benefit from a kinesthetic approach to learning lower-case letters. Extensive research has shown that students are more likely to confuse objects and symbols that share visual and/or auditory samenesses, such as *b* and *d*.[8]

In solving simple computation problems, such as 24 + 13, first-graders learn that they can start with the bottom number in the units column or with the top number: 4 + 3 equals 7, and so does 3 + 4. The sameness they note is that these problems can be worked in either direction, from top to bottom or the reverse. Soon thereafter come subtraction problems, such as 24 – 13. Students can still apply the sameness learned in addition, thinking of the difference between 4 and 3 or between 3 and 4 and always subtracting the smaller number from the larger. However, when students encounter a problem such as 74 – 15, applying the sameness noted earlier leads them to subtract the smaller from the larger number and come up with the answer 61. Such a mistake is a sensible application of a mislearned sameness.

The next example of learning an unintended sameness comes from second-grade spelling. Hispanic students in the primary grades were doing very well in a basal spelling program. Such words as *site, kite, bite, high, sigh,* and *eye* were introduced on Monday and practiced in the same order until a test on Friday. A consultant noted that the students scored very well on the Friday test; the class average was over 80% correct. However, he suspected that the students had learned some samenesses that were not intended by the publisher or the teacher: for the first three words the students wrote the letter for the first sound and then wrote *ite;* for the next two words, they wrote the letter for the first sound and then wrote *igh;* for *eye,* they simply remembered how to spell the word.

> **If there is lots of numbers, I add. If there are only two numbers with lots of parts, I subtract.**

To test for this unintended sameness, the consultant had the teacher present the same six words again—but in a different order. The class average fell to below 40% correct. The word spelled correctly most often was *eye,* the one odd word that the students had to remember how to spell because it didn't fit a pattern, didn't exhibit a sameness.

Or consider the following example from reading. Many basal readers restrict vocabulary during grades 1 and 2 to a few hundred words and emphasize reading for meaning, using context clues and pictures. The sameness that students learn from reading basal stories is to memorize a few hundred words, relying on pictures and context. In most third-grade basals, however, there are few pictures and many, many more words—too many for low-achieving students to memorize. The inappropriate sameness learned by low-achieving students isn't revealed until third grade, when they "blossom" into remedial readers.

Or consider a fourth-grader's strategy for solving math word problems, which she derived from a sameness she found in the word problems she had previously encountered. This is her description of the rules she learned: "If there is lots of numbers, I add. If there are only two numbers with lots of parts, I subtract. But if there is just two numbers, and one is a little harder than the other, then it is a hard problem, so I divide if they come out even, but if they don't, I multiply." A unique strategy, perhaps, but one that had proved successful in her experience.

Let me offer a final example from the area of study skills. The student who learns to find a word in a glossary by searching page by page, beginning with the first page, will quickly give up on using a dictionary. Treating a dictionary in the same way as a glossary— turning page by page from the beginning—proves to be too slow, particularly if the object of the search is the word *zenith*.

These examples are from elementary schools, and it can be difficult to appreciate the universality of the problem because the "samenesses" are all so familiar. In the next example, imagine that you are the learner, looking for samenesses. The concept is *Zug*. Study the examples, and then solve the two problems.

a. Zug 20
        15
         5

b. Zug 24
        18
         6

c. Zug 21
         7
        ___

d. Zug   8
         2
        ___

If you filled in the blanks with 14 and 6, you noted an "incorrect" sameness. *Zug* does not mean: "Find the difference between these numbers." I'll return to Zug below.

INDUCING INTENDED SAMENESSES

The brain's search for samenesses has little regard for the intentions of educators. The examples above show some of the ways in which students often learn unintended samenesses. However, recognizing the brain's search for samenesses does more than explain student misconceptions. It can also guide the development of more effective curricular activities. The goal is to develop activities that help students learn important samenesses. Such activities should also keep students from learning inappropriate samenesses, and they should call attention to unintended samenesses that students are likely to learn.

To reduce confusion between *b* and *d*, for example, the curriculum designer can separate the introduction of these letters over time.[9] When *d* is introduced some time later, a teacher could stress the differences between *b* and *d*, using visual discrimination tasks before introducing auditory discrimination tasks.[10]

In preparing students for subtraction that involves borrowing, the curriculum designer can emphasize the ways in which borrowing problems are *not* the same as addition problems and simple subtraction problems. To highlight these differences, the designer might present a series of simple problems.

$$
\begin{array}{cccc}
1 & 7 & 5 & 2 \\
\underline{-7} & \underline{-1} & \underline{-2} & \underline{-5}
\end{array}
$$

Students would be told that they had to subtract the *bottom* number from the *top* number. The students would then cross out the problems that they couldn't work and write the answers to the problems that they could work. This activity reduces the sameness between addition and subtraction by sensitizing students to the consequences of having a smaller number on top.

Let's revisit Zug. Study examples *e* through *j*, which are all examples of Zug. Then try *c* and *d* from the previous set of Zug problems.

$$
\begin{array}{ll}
\text{e.}\ \ \begin{array}{r} 25 \\ \underline{15} \\ 5 \end{array} & \text{f.}\ \ \begin{array}{r} 25 \\ \underline{10} \\ 5 \end{array} \\
\\
\text{g.}\ \ \begin{array}{r} 20 \\ \underline{10} \\ 10 \end{array} & \text{h.}\ \ \begin{array}{r} 20 \\ \underline{8} \\ 4 \end{array} \\
\\
\text{i.}\ \ \begin{array}{r} 6 \\ \underline{2} \\ 2 \end{array} & \text{j.}\ \ \begin{array}{r} 16 \\ \underline{8} \\ 8 \end{array}
\end{array}
$$

The correct answers for *c* and *d* above are 7 and 2. *Zug* means: "Find the greatest common factor." Examples *e* through *j* are better for teaching the concept of Zug because those examples were constructed following research-based guidelines for teaching samenesses.

SELECTING AND SEQUENCING EXAMPLES

Among the guidelines for selecting and sequencing examples (such as those for Zug) are the following:

• Select examples that preclude unintended samenesses.[11] In examples e, f, h, and i, the answers do not equal the number that results from subtracting the lower number from the upper, and the unintended similarity is precluded.

• Present minimally different examples to highlight unintended samenesses that students need to reject.[12] In examples *e* and *f*, the top numbers and the answers are the same, but the answers cannot result from subtracting. Such minimally different examples are relatively easy to compare.

I will illustrate these two principles by reporting the results of a study that compared a videodisc curriculum designed to teach fractions according to research-based guidelines with the best basal math program that could be identified.[13]

The first principle—eliminating unintended samenesses—can prevent students from forming misconceptions. Basal math texts introduce fractions as parts of a pie: $^1/_3$, $^2/_3$, $^3/_3$, $^1/_4$, $^2/_4$, and so on. The text for the following year introduces mixed numbers, but the fraction is still less than one, still just part of a single pie. Thus students have at least two years to "learn" that a fraction always represents a portion of a pie. They can deduce (and be reinforced for deducing) the "fact" that all fractions are the same in that they represent part of a whole. In the third year, students encounter such fractions as $^4/_3$, a new wrinkle that causes bewilderment for low-achieving students. To deal with this seeming violation of the sameness they have learned, many of these students draw a pie with four parts and shade three of them.

This confusion was reduced in the research-based curriculum by presenting a full range of examples (e.g., $^2/_3$ and $^5/_2$) from the outset. Students were given this rule to explain how all fractions are the same: "The number on the bottom of the fraction tells how many parts in each group. The top number tells how many parts we have." This rule applies equally well to improper ($5/2$) and proper ($2/3$) fractions.

The second principle—sequencing minimally different examples—can alert learners to unintended samenesses. The National Assessment of Educational Progress found that many students had learned an unintended sameness about denominators in problems involving the addition fractions.[14] The students had learned to "do what the sign says." This sameness derives from students' experiences with whole numbers and with multiplying fractions. When students multiply $1/3 \times 1/2$, the denominators are multiplied. When students apply this sameness to addition ($1/3 + 1/2$), they add the denominators to get $2/5$.

> The guidelines for selecting and sequencing examples are important tools for educators, but they are not sufficient by themselves.

The basal program we studied does not deal with this unintended sameness. It teaches adding and subtracting fractions in one unit and multiplying and dividing fractions in another. Students receive no instruction or guided practice in distinguishing addition of fractions from multiplication of fractions.

The research-based curriculum, on the other hand, addresses this unintended sameness directly. Students are told that, when they add or subtract, they simply copy the denominator in the answer. Adding $2/3$ and $1/3$ is like adding two apples and one apple. The answer is three *thirds* (or apples).

The research-based curriculum presents minimally different examples: $2/3 + 1/3$ is transformed through videodisc animation into $2/3 \times 1/3$ by rotating the + sign to make a $\times$ sign. By encountering minimally different problems, students have opportunities to decide what to do when they add and what to do when they multiply.

The guidelines for selecting and sequencing examples are important tools for educators, but they are not sufficient by themselves. Particularly at the secondary level, more sophisticated tools are also needed, such as multistep procedures and unifying principles.

Multipstep Procedures

A multistep procedure requires students to carry out the same sequence of actions in solving a variety of problems. The explicit procedure informs students that two problems are the same because they can be solved by following the same steps.

The research on story grammar illustrates the use of such a multistep procedure.[15] Many short stories adhere to a set structure: a major character encounters a problem, acts to overcome that problem, and ultimately resolves it in some way. Students can learn to identify first the main character, then the problem, then the actions taken to resolve the problem, and finally the ultimate resolution. Students learn that, because many stories share this structure, the story grammar questions are useful in "making sense" of stories.

With this type of summary, the children could have discussed the theme of the story intelligently.

The need to teach students an explicit multistep procedure for comprehending even simple stories was driven home when I observed a first-grade teacher working with a reading group. She asked a hodgepodge of literal and inferential comprehension questions as the children read "The Boy Who Cried Wolf." The students were learning the sameness that the purpose of reading is to remember isolated facts about a passage. If the students had learned a multistep procedure based on story grammar, they could have identified the boy's problem as boredom, his solution as crying wolf (which did relieve his boredom), and the resolution as no one believing him when he cried wolf in earnest. With this type of summary, the children could have discussed the theme of the story intelligently. More important, they could apply the same procedure to many other stories. A more sophisticated story grammar that incorporates twists of plot, clues about characters, and so on has also been taught successfully to high school students.[16]

Unifying Principles

A unifying principle is another way of showing how things are the same. Identifying unifying principles is particularly important in the sciences and social sciences, in which students are inundated by a great number of seemingly unrelated facts and concepts. According to one estimate, students would need to learn a new biological concept every two minutes in order to cover the content of a high school biology textbook. A typical biology textbook introduces twice as many new concepts in a year as the American Foreign Language Association recommends for foreign-language learners. Most students try to remember some of the new vocabulary in biology—at least until after they take the next test.

One way of handling this information overload and the attendant misconceptions about the nature of science is first to identify the underlying principles of a discipline. The concepts necessary to understand the underlying principles can be taught initially. Then students can learn about the unifying principles themselves—and finally about the application of the principles.[17] For example, earth science covers a wide variety of phenomena in the solid earth, in the oceans, and in the atmosphere. Yet textbooks do not emphasize the underlying principle of convection. Prerequisite to understanding convection—the circulation of heat through a medium—is the understanding of many other concepts: heating and cooling, the implications for expansion and contraction, subsequent rising and sinking, and, finally, areas of high and low atmospheric pressure.

After the concept of convection has been taught, it can be used to explain ocean currents, air currents, and many phenomena in the solid earth. All of these phenomena are the same in that they are caused at least partly by convection.

Figure 1 graphically depicts convection cells in the solid earth and shows how they account for plate tectonics, which in turn explains granite mountains, volcanoes, earthquakes, mid-oceanic trenches, and so forth. The crust of the earth actually rides on top of the convection cells illustrated in Figure 1. At point A, two sections of the crust come together at a subduction zone, where the crust of the ocean floor goes under the continental crust, causing earthquakes, rift valleys, and volcanoes. At point B, the ocean crust is pulled apart by two convection cells, causing trenches and volcanoes. The large sections of the earth's crust that ride on these convection cells form the "plates" referred to in *plate tectonics*. The unifying principle of convection reveals a fundamental sameness in many phenomena in the ocean, atmosphere, and solid earth. Instruction along these lines leads to a more sophisticated comprehension of science principles and their application.[18]

Figure 1

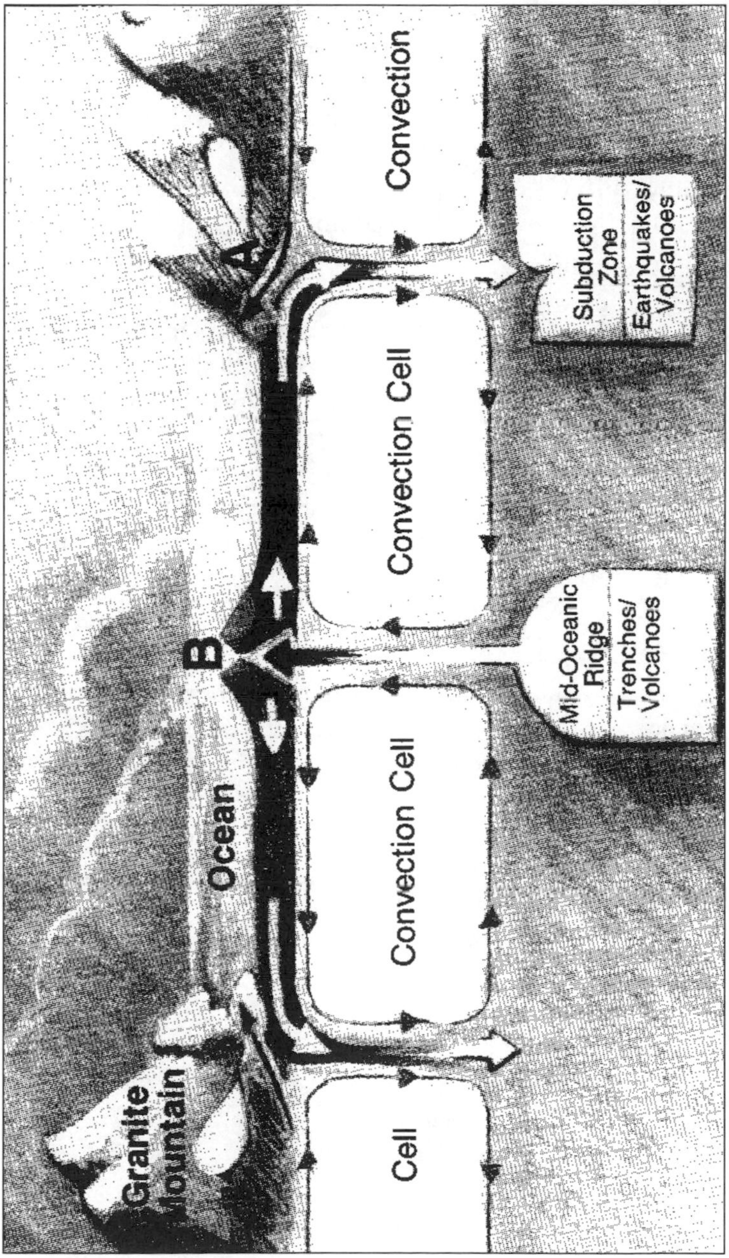

PRACTICE AND REVIEW

Though critical for the acquisition of new content, learning the appropriate samenesses does not touch on many other important aspects of learning. For example, if students are to retain newly acquired samenesses, they should practice until they can consistently respond correctly.[19] In the basal math program critiqued above, the skill of finding the least common multiple was introduced in one lesson, disappeared for seven lessons, was then reviewed in one lesson, disappeared again for six lessons, and then appeared in the context of adding and subtracting fractions with unlike denominators. Two exposures over the course of 15 lessons are not sufficient for even students of average ability to acquire and retain a concept. The research-based curriculum introduced this skill and gave students practice in eight consecutive lessons. Then, in the very next lesson, students applied the skill in problems with unlike denominators.

> The conundrum of how to respond to individual differences in learning and remembering has haunted educators for decades.

SUMMING UP

Developing skills for learning and remembering are important goals for schools. The conundrum of how to respond to individual differences in learning and remembering has haunted educators for decades. As new theories from other disciplines make their way into education, they often play a part in the evolution of various educational responses to the challenge of individual differences in learning. Gerald Edelman's work on the overarching capacity of the human brain to categorize in connected ways has direct implications for educators.

This capacity to categorize may also be a key to understanding individual differences. Bright, intuitive learners may be capable of categorizing and recategorizing rapidly and flexibly, without the need for an instructional environment that emphasizes important samenesses and "warns" about unintended ones. These students can "figure out" important samenesses without getting seriously misled.

Consider the following example of teaching students to rewrite fractions. It begins with such semiconcrete representations as this:

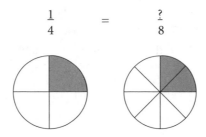

The pictures are assumed to develop the concept that $1/4$ can also be written as $2/8$, because the same area of both circles is shaded. The inappropriate sameness implied by problems of this type is that the answer can be determined by counting the shaded parts, ignoring everything else. This misconception can easily be demonstrated by asking students to solve a problem such as $2/3 - 1/6$. There are no shaded parts to count.

The intuitive learner, left without parts to count, will look for other samenesses that will yield an answer, a process similar to deducing that *Zug* does not mean *subtract*. Knowing when to search for new samenesses, how to generate alternative samenesses, and how to evaluate those samenesses are the hallmarks of the intuitive learner.

The challenge for educators is quite different with low-achieving students. One problem is to help those students become more "intuitive." Yet designing activities toward that end must not be the only tactic, partly because documented successes in creating such activities for low-achieving student are rare. The other tactic was illustrated above: designing a learning environment to maximize the likelihood that students will learn important samenesses. For example, in teaching low-achieving students to rewrite fractions, one important sameness can be expressed as a rule: "Multiplying one side of an equation by 1 or by a fraction equal to 1 does not change the value of that side." Thus, when students are asked to rewrite $2/3$ as a fraction with 15 in the denominator, they will understand that they must multiply $2/3$ by a fraction that is equivalent to 1 and that will convert the 3 in the denominator to a 15. Thus their choice must be $5/5$. The rule about multiplying by 1 derives from one of the great unifying principles of mathematics: identity elements for mathematical operations do not alter relationships.

A different type of equality underlies the interest of educators in individual differences—not equal treatment, not even equal outcomes, but equal opportunity to learn and flourish in school. Determining the nature of those opportunities is education's grail. Differing theories of the brain can be interpreted as supporting different instructional approaches, and choices among these approaches should be based as much as possible on their effects on students.

This seeming truism is actually very difficult to put into practice.[20] For example, the notion that individual learning styles stem from relative strengths and weaknesses of brain functions was very popular in special education in the 1960s and 1970s. However, numerous research studies documented seemingly insurmountable flaws in the way in which special education applied that notion.[21] Among these flaws are the following: (1) measures for identifying students' learning styles are not reliable (e.g., a student might exhibit a visual strength on the day of testing but a visual weakness on a different day); (2) relationships between learning-style strengths and academic performance are weak (e.g., the correlation between students' scores on tests of learning styles and their scores on reading tests was lower than the correlation between students' scores on reading tests and their scores on tests of math computation); and (3) instruction matched to students' learning styles had relatively weak effects on academic performance (e.g., instruction to improve visual functioning didn't appreciably improve reading performance). As noted in a recent *Kappan* article, the research base on learning styles outside of special education is also open to question.[22]

On the other hand, the educational principles outlined in this article have been subjected to large-scale evaluations in elementary reading and mathematics.[23] Small-scale research studies at the University of Oregon have also been conducted in various secondary subjects, including physical science, law, critical reading, syllogistic reasoning, math word problems, problem solving and literary analysis.[24] The point I wish to leave with [this book's] readers is that arguing by analogy from brain research to education provides only a rationale for an approach. The actual effect of the approach on students is what is crucial. Edelman's new research on the brain provides a strong rationale for the analysis of sameness, which has extensive research support.

NOTES

1. Marie Carbo, "Reading Styles Research: 'What Works' Isn't Always Phonics," *Phi Delta Kappan,* February 1987, pp. 431–35.

2. Gerald Edelman, *Neural Darwinism: The Theory of Neuronal Group Selection* (New York: Basic Books, 1987).

3. Israel Rosenfield, *The Invention of Memory* (New York: Basic Books, 1988), p. 10.

4. Ibid., p. 112.

5. Ibid, p. 189.

6. Ibid, p. 192.

7. Ibid, p. 149.

8. Douglas W. Carnine, "Two Letter Discrimination Sequences: High-Confusion Alternatives First Versus Low-Confusion Alternatives First," *Journal of Reading Behavior,* vol. 12, 1980, pp. 29–40.

9. Douglas W. Carnine, "Similar Sound Separation and Cumulative 'Introduction in Learning Letter-Sound Correspondences," *Journal of Educational Research,* vol. 69, 1976, pp. 368–72.

10. Douglas W. Carnine, "Reducing Training Problems Associated with Visually and Auditorily Similar Consequences," *Journal of Learning Disabilities,* vol. 14, 1981, pp. 276–79.

11. Douglas W. Carnine, "Relationships Between Stimulus Variation and the Formation of Misconceptions," *Journal of Educational Research,* vol. 74, 1980, pp. 106–10.

12. Douglas W. Carnine, "Three Procedures for Presenting Minimally Different Positive and Negative Instances," *Journal of Educational Psychology,* vol. 72, 1980, pp. 452–56; and Alex C. Granzin and Douglas W. Carnine, "Child Performance on Discrimination Tasks: Effects of Amount of Stimulus Variation," *Journal of Experimental Child Psychology,* vol. 24, 1977, pp. 332–42.

13. The research-based curriculum was *Mastering Fractions* (Washington, D.C.: Systems Impact, Inc., 1985). The full study is reported in Bernadette Kelly, Douglas Carnine, Russell Gersten, and Bonnie Grossen, "The Effectiveness of Videodisc Instruction in Teaching Fractions to Learning Handicapped and Remedial High School Students," *Journal of Special Education Technology,* vol. 8, 1986, pp. 5–17.

14. Thomas P. Carpenter et al., "Notes from National Assessment: Addition and Multiplication with Fractions," *Arithmetic Teacher,* vol. 23, 1976, pp. 137–42.

15. Douglas W. Carnine and Diane Kinder, "Teaching Low-Performance Students to Apply Generative and Schema Strategies to Narrative and Expository Material," *Remedial and Special Education*, vol. 6, 1985, pp. 20–30.

16. Joe Dimino, Russell Gersten, Douglas Carnine, and Geneva Blake, "Using Story Grammar to Promote Ninth-Graders' Comprehension of Literature," *Elementary School Journal*, in press; and Dana Gurney, Russell Gersten, Joe Dimino, and Douglas Carnine, "Story Grammar: Effective Learning Instruction for High School Students with Learning Disabilities," *Journal of Learning Disabilities*, in press.

17. Alan Hofmeister, Siegfried Engelmann, and Douglas Carnine, "Developing and Validating Science Education Videodiscs," *Journal of Research in Science Teaching*, vol. 26, 1989, pp. 665–77.

18. John Woodward, *Developing Schema in Earth Science* (Eugene: University of Oregon, Technical Report No. 89-3, 1989).

19. Craig Darch, Douglas Carnine, and Russell Gersten, "Explicit Instruction in Mathematics Problem Solving," *Journal of Educational Research*, vol. 77, 1984, pp. 350–59.

20. Douglas W. Carnine, "Overcoming Barriers to Student Achievement," in S. J. Samuels and P. David Pearson, eds., *Changing School Reading Programs* (Newark, Del.: International Reading Association, 1988), pp. 59–91.

21. For a review of the research on this topic, see Kenneth Kavelle and Steven Forness, "Substance over Style: Assessing the Efficacy of Modality Testing and Teaching," *Exceptional Children*, vol. 54, 1987, pp. 228–39.

22. Steven A. Stahl, "Is There Evidence to Support Matching Reading Styles and Initial Reading Methods? A Reply to Carbo," *Phi Delta Kappan*, December 1988, pp. 317–22.

23. Linda Stebbins et al., *Education as Experimentation: A Planned Variation Model*, 4 vols. (Cambridge, Mass.: Abt Associates, 1977).

24. Hofmeister, Engelmann, and Carnine, op. cit.; Glenn Fielding, Ed Kameenui, and Russell Gersten, "A Comparison of an Inquiry-Oriented and a Direct Instruction Approach to Teaching Legal Problem Solving to Secondary School Students," *Journal of Educational Research*, vol. 76, 1983, pp. 287–93; William Patching et al., "Direct Instruction in Critical Reading," *Reading Research Quarterly*, vol. 18, 1983, pp. 406–18; Maria Collins and Douglas Carnine, "Evaluating the Field Test Revision Process by Comparing Two Versions of a Reasoning Skills CAI Program," *Journal of Learning Disabilities*, vol. 21, 1988, pp. 375–79; Darch, Carnine and Gersten, op. cit.; John Woodward, Douglas Carnine, and Russell Gersten, "Teaching Problem Solving Through a Computer Simulation," *American Educational Research Journal*, vol. 25, 1988, pp. 72–86; and Dimino, Gersten, Carnine, and Blake, op. cit.

RECOMMENDED READINGS

Caine, Renate Nummela, and Geoffrey Caine. *Education on the Edge of Possibility*. Alexandria, VA: Association for Supervision and Curriculum Development, 1997.
A case study of an attempt to apply brain research discoveries to classroom life. It's a thoughtful discussion of a very difficult task, but an optimistic one as it suggests how the process finally might be accomplished.

Dehaene, Stanislas. *The Number Sense: How the Mind Creates Mathematics*. New York: Oxford, 1997.
A marvelous book! Dehaene's work is described in the article that begins on page 129. This book is a wealth of useful information for all educators—and a *must read* for all who focus on math education.

Jackendoff, Ray. *Patterns in the Mind: Language and Human Nature*. New York: Basic Books, 1994.
An excellent, stimulating, nontechnical discussion of the broad range of language by a noted scholar in the field. This book provides very useful background information for educators, all of whom are language teachers in one way or another.

Solso, Robert L., editor. *Mind and Brain Sciences in the 21st Century*. Cambridge, MA: MIT Press, 1997.
The projections of seventeen noted brain scientists about where their specialty will probably be in the twenty-first century. Projections range from the specific to the general to the whimsical, but all provide much food for thought for educators, whose future depends at least in part on where the brain sciences take us. A very thoughtful and thought-provoking book.

Authors

Ron Brandt is the author, coauthor, or editor of over a dozen books related to education. A former executive director of Association for Supervision and Curriculum Development, he now serves as *Educational Leadership*'s executive editor emeritus.

Douglas Carnine is Professor of Education at the University of Oregon and the director of the National Center to Improve the Tools of Educators. He has over 100 scholarly publications. He is the consulting editor or editorial board member for eight journals and has presented at over 100 conferences worldwide.

Shannon Brownlee is a senior writer for *U.S. News & World Report*. The recipient of several awards, including the 1987 American Institute of Physics Award and the 1990 General Motors Cancer Research Foundation Award, she also received the first place prize from the Sigma-Tau Foundation for a story on Alzheimer's disease.

Kathy Checkley is a staff writer for *Update* and has assisted in the development of the Association for Supervision and Curriculum Development's CD-ROM *Exploring Our Multiple Intelligences*.

Jo Ann C. Gutin, an anthropologist and science writer, is the winner of the 1995 National Book Critics Circle Award for criticism. A contributor to *Discover* magazine, she has written on topics such as the brain and the evolution of language.

Rebecca Jones is senior editor of *The American School Board Journal* and the author of fourteen children's books.

Barbara Kantrowitz, a senior editor at *Newsweek,* has an extensive background writing on topics such as education, technology, and the family. The coauthor of *The Ultimate Baby Catalog,* she has received numerous awards, including the 1992 National Education Reporting Award from the Education Writers Association and the 1994 Front Page award from the Newswomen's Club of New York.

Robert Kunzig, *Discover*'s European editor, lives in France and specializes in scientific and technological subjects, including oceanography and space.

David Moursund is a professor in the University of Oregon's College of Education. The founder of the International Council for Computers in Education, which became the International Society for Technology in Education, he serves as its executive officer. He is the author or coauthor of more than 30 books and numerous articles on computer technology in education.

John O'Neil is a book acquisitions editor for the Association for Supervision and Curriculum Development (ASCD). In addition, he is a contributing editor for ASCD's journal, *Educational Leadership.*

Robert Sternberg is IBM Professor of Psychology and Education in the Department of Psychology at Yale University. The author of more than 300 books and articles, he has won numerous awards, including the Distinguished Scientific Award for an Early Career Contribution to Psychology and the Boyd R. McCandless Young Scientist Award from the American Psychological Association.

Robert Sylwester, Ph.D., is a professor emeritus at the University of Oregon, College of Education, Eugene, OR 97403. He is a leader in how brain research affects teaching and learning. He recently authored *A Celebration of Neurons: An Educator's Guide to the Human Brain.*

Pat Wingert, a general assignment correspondent for *Newsweek*'s Washington bureau, covers issues related to education, children, and welfare reform. The recipient of numerous awards, she shared the 1992 Education Writers Association Award for *Newsweek*'s cover story, "The 10 Best Schools in the World," and its 1989 award for her cover story on how kids learn.

Acknowledgments

Grateful acknowledgment is made to the following authors and agents for their permission to reprint copyrighted materials.

SECTION 1

Association for Supervision and Curriculum Development (ASCD) for "On Using Knowledge About Our Brain: A Conversation with Bob Sylwester," by Ron Brandt. From *Educational Leadership*, March 1997, pp. 16–19. © 1997 by ASCD. All rights reserved. Reprinted with permission.

National School Boards Association for "Smart Brains," by Rebecca Jones. From *The American School Board Journal*, November 1995, pp. 22–26. © 1995 by the National School Boards Association. All rights reserved. Reprinted with permission.

SECTION 2

Association for Supervision and Curriculum Development (ASCD) for "On Emotional Intelligence: A Conversation with Daniel Goleman," by John O'Neil. From *Educational Leadership*, September 1996, pp. 6–11. © 1996 by ASCD. All rights reserved. Reprinted with permission.

Association for Supervision and Curriculum Development (ASCD) for "How Emotions Affect Learning," by Robert Sylwester. From *Educational Leadership*, October 1994, pp. 60–65. © 1994 by ASCD. All rights reserved. Reprinted with permission.

SECTION 3

SECTION 4

Discover magazine for "A Brain That Talks," by Jo Ann C. Gutin. From *Discover,* June 1996, pp. 83–90. © 1996 by Jo Ann C. Gutin. All rights reserved. Reprinted with permission of *Discover* magazine.

Newsweek, Inc. for "Why Andy Couldn't Read," by Pat Wingert and Barbara Kantrowitz. From *Newsweek,* October 27, 1997, pp. 57–64. © 1997, Newsweek, Inc. All rights reserved. Reprinted with permission.

Discover magazine for "A Head for Numbers," by Robert Kunzig. From *Discover,* July 1997, pp. 108–115. © 1997 by Robert Kunzig. All rights reserved. Reprinted with permission of *Discover* magazine.

Douglas Carnine for "New Research on the Brain: Implications for Instruction," by Douglas Carnine. From *Phi Delta Kappa,* vol. 71, no. 5, January 1990, pp. 372–377. © 1990 by Douglas Carnine. All rights reserved. Reprinted with permission.

Index

Ability tests, 72
Abstract reasoning, connections
    between music and, 15–16
Academic success, relationship
    between emotional skills and,
    22
Achenbach, Thomas, 25
Addition, 136, 146
Aggression
    neurobiology of, 41–48
    roots of violent, 42–44
Agraphia, 132
Amygdala, 35
Amygdala complex, 34
Analysis, 74
Analytical thinking, 12
Approaching behaviors, 36
Artificial intelligence, 91–92
Assessment tools, multiple
    intelligences in creating, 68
Attention, 1
Attention deficit disorder (ADD),
    124
Attention research, 6
Auden, W. H., 55
Auditory timing errors, 14
Autism, 3

Balzer-Martin, Lynn A., 125
Basal ganglia, 136
Bioelectronic learning, 81–87
Biology, placing emphasis on, 6
Bodily kinesthetic intelligence, 63
Brain
    anatomy of, 83
    development of, 83–85
    effects of electronic media on
        developing, 81–87
    MRI images of, 13
    new techniques in scanning of,
        106–107
    our, and social systems, 44–46
    regulatory centers for emotional
        response, 24
    search for samenesses, 147–149
    using knowledge on, 3–8
Brain-compatible classrooms, 5–6,
    10–11
Brain hemisphere studies, 4
Brain-imaging technology, v,
    112–113
Brain opiates, 53
Brain research, 4, 10–11
    advances in, 3
    benefits of, 11–13

connection between education
    and, 14
implications for teaching,
    143–156
Brain sciences, v–vi, 2
Brain stem, 33–35
Brandt, Ron, 3–8
Bregman, Joanne, 124–125
Broca's area, 107, 114
Brownlee, Shannon, 51–55
Bruer, John, 11

Calvin, William, 4
Carnine, Douglas, 143–156
Carter, Sue, 51, 52
Categorization, 144, 154
Cerebral cortex, 33, 35–36
Checkley, Kathy, 61–70
Chronic stress, 32
Cloning, 1
Cognitive science
    developments in, 29–30
    research in, 48
Cognitive tasks, v
Cohen, Laurent, 129, 135–137, 139
Common sense, 112
Common sensorium, 112
Computational thought processes,
    new perspectives on, 103–159
Computer-assisted learning (CAL),
    94, 95
Computerized research technolo-
    gies, vii
Computer-managed instruction
    (CMI), 95
Computer productivity tools, 93–94
Computer technology, vi
Computing power, student access
    to, 90
Connectivity, 90–91
Convection, 152
Cooperative learning, 92
Cortex, 35

Cortical neurons, 83–84
Cortisol, 32
Creative domains, 72
Creativity, 12, 74, 77
Cultural memory, 81–82
Curriculum content, 96–97

Dale, Anders, 113
Darwin, Charles, 62
Declarative memory, 34
DeFries, John, 125
Dehaene, Stanislas, 104, 129, 131,
    135–137, 139
Denckla, Martha Bridge, 122
DeVries, Courtney, 53
Dewey, John, 10, 29, 38
Diamond, Marian, 16
Digital competence, 8
Distance effect, 131
DNA, 1, 108
Drugs, 31
    in stimulating serotonin system,
    47
Dyscalculia, 123–124
Dyslexia, 6, 14, 120–121, 122

Edelman, Gerald, 143, 154
Education
    challenges in, vi–viii
    connection between brain
        research and, 14
    costs of, as closed system, 71–72
    future of information technol-
        ogy in, 89–100
    importance of emotion on, 29
    inservice teacher, 98–99
    just-in-time, 95
    physical, 73
    preservice, of teachers, 97
    of whole child, 29
Educational system, changing
    capability of informal, 95
Einstein, Albert, vi

Electroencephalography (EEG), 113
Electronic media, effects of, on
    developing brain, 81–87
Electron microscopes, 3
Emotional intelligence, 21–28
Emotional literacy
    curriculum of, 27
    teaching, 26–27
Emotional skills, relationship
    between academic success
    and, 22
Emotions
    definition of, 19
    educational applications of
      research, 36–38
    emergence and importance of,
      19–57
    impact of, on learning, 29–38
    problems in studying, 19
Endorphins, 32, 53
Epilepsy, 4
Erikson, Erik, 69
Ethical constraints on research, 1
Euphoria, 32
Existential intelligence, 64
Expert systems, capabilities of, 91

Finger agnosia, 132
Fitzpatrick, Susan, 12, 14
Flexibility, 77
Folklore knowledge, 2
Fractions, teaching students to
    rewrite, 154–155
Frontal lobes, 36
Functional magnetic resonance
    imaging (fMRI), 3, 10, 113, 122

Galton, Francis, 130–131
Gardner, Howard, 10, 20, 59, 60,
    61–70
Gauss, Carl Friedrich, 138
Genetic engineering, 1, 5
Genetics, role in brain
    development, 84
Gerstmann, Josef, 132

Gerstmann's syndrome, 140
Ghettoizing, 27
Goleman, Daniel, 20, 21–28
Gutin, Jo Ann C., 105–117

Hippocampus, 34
Hormonal systems, 20
Hormones, 31
Hubel, David, 15
Human intelligence, study of, 69
Hunger, impact of learning on, 16
Hypermedia, 92–93
Hypothalamus, 34–35, 35

Individual differences, interest of
    educators in, 156
Information technology, future of,
    in education, 89
Inherited learning disorders,
    identifying, 125
Inservice teacher education, 98–99
Intelligence
    definition of, 61–62
    emotional, 21–28
    strengthening, 65
Intelligent behavior, 4
Intended samenesses, inducing,
    147–149
Internet connectivity, 94
Interpersonal intelligence, 63
Intrapersonal intelligence, 63
IQ, 21, 64–65
IQ test, 64–65

Johnson, David, 48
Johnson, Roger, 48
Jones, Rebecca, 9–17
"Just-in-time" education, 95

Kagan, Jerome, 24
Kantrowitz, Barbara, 119–128
Keverne, Barry, 54
Knowledge, using, on brain, 3–8
Kunzig, Robert, 129–141

Lab School of Washington, 126
Landauer, Thomas, 131
Language ability, 106
Language arts, 74
Language development, 107–110,
    114–117
Language evolution, 107–108
Language hemisphere, 135
Larynx, 115–116
Learning
    bioelectronic, 81–87
    computer-assisted, 94, 95
    cooperative, 92
    impact of emotions on, 29–38
    impact of hunger on, 16
    physiology of, 12
    technology-enhanced, 95–96
    types of, 13
    whole, 6
Learning Disabilities Association,
    121
Learning-disabilities programs,
    119–128
Learning disorders, identifying
    inherited, 125
Learning opportunities, importance
    of early, 15
Learning styles
    distinction between multiple
        intelligences and, 68–69
    individual, 156
Learning task, orientation of, 7
Left hemisphere, 36
Lerner, Janet, 124
Limbic system, 33–35
Linguistic intelligence, 63
Linguistics, 123
Localization, 143–144
Localization of function, doctrine
    of, 143
Logical-mathematical intelligence,
    63
Long-term memory, 85–86

Love, 51–55
Lyon, G. Reid, 123

Magnetic resonance imaging,
    functional, 3, 10, 113, 122
Magnetic resonance imaging
    (MRI) scanners, 138
Magnetoencephalography (MEG),
    113
"Marshmallow" study at Stanford,
    22
Mathematics, 74
    disabilities in, 124
McGuinness, Diane, 127
Memory, 74
    cultural, 81–82
    long-term, 85–86
    personal, 81
    procedural, 33–34
    short-term, 85
    storage of, in brain, 9
    working, 23
Memory process, 6
Memory systems, 85–86
Mertz, Suzanne, 127–128
Microcomputers
    capabilities of, 90
    in schools, 90
Mind control, 46
Minskoff, Esther, 126
Moursund, David, 60, 89–100
Moyer, Robert, 131
Multiple intelligences, 7, 20, 61–70
    in creating assessment tools, 68
    implementing theory of, 66–67
    influence on teaching methods,
        66
    myths about theory of, 68–69
Multiplication, 136
Multipstep procedures, 151
Music, connections between
    abstract reasoning and, 15–16
Musical intelligence, 63

National Assessment of Educational Progress, 150
Naturalist intelligence, 62, 63, 64
Neocortex, 36
Neurobiology of self-esteem and aggression, 41–48
Neurons, v, 4
Neuropeptides, 31
Neuroscience, 9–17
    practical applications of, 5
Neurotransmitters, v, 34
    studies of, 20
Noradrenaline neurotransmitters, 34
Number line, 129–141, 135–137
Numerical disability, 139
Nutrition
    importance of good, 16
    in stimulating serotonin system, 47

O'Neil, John, 21–28
Opiate endorphins, 34
Opiates, 54
Oxytocin, 20, 51, 52–53

Panksepp, Jack, 54
Pech, Rose, 127
Peptides, 31–33
Personal identities, developing, 20
Personal memory, 81
Petersen, Steven, 11, 12–13, 14
Pheromones, 35
Phonics, 123, 127
Phonological awareness deficit, 123
Physical education, 73
Polymodal cortex, 112
Porges, Stephen, 54–55
Portfolio assessments, 48
Position emission tomography (PET), 10, 138
Practical domains, 72
Practicality, 74

Preservice education of teachers, 97
Primary motor region, 132
Procedural memory, 33–34
Productivity tools
    for students, 93–94
    for teachers, 94
Prozac, 43, 46, 47

Rauscher, Frances, 16
Reading, problems in learning how, 119–128
Recategorization, 144
Response systems, 86–87
Reticular formation, 33
Right hemisphere, 36
Rosenfield, Israel, 143–144, 145
Rote memorization, 11

Samenesses, brain's search for, 147–149
Sarason, Seymour, 89
Scaffolding, 13–14
Scheibel, Arnold, 11
Schneider, Walter, 10
School-home connection, 99–100
Science, 74
Scientific discovery, practical applications from, 2–18
Selecting and sequencing examples, 149–150
Self-esteem, 38
    in hierarchy, 41–42
    neurobiology of, 41–48
Semantics, 114
Sensory lobes, 36
Sereno, Claudia, 104, 113
Sereno, Marty, 105–117
Serotonin, 3, 20, 42, 43, 44, 45, 47
Shaw, Gordon, 16
Shaywitz, Sally, 120
Short-term memory, 85
Social identities, developing, 20

Social studies, 74
Social systems, our brain and, 44–46
Space-time demands, 35
Spatial intelligence, 63
Spatial-temporal skills, 16
Sperry, Roger, 4
Spoken-language problems, 123
Sternberg, Robert J., 60, 71–78
Subtraction, 136
Sylwester, Robert, 3–8, 29–38,
    41–48, 81–87
Synaptic gap, 44
Syntax, 114

Teachers
    productivity tools of, 94
    teaching future, 7–8
    training of, 91–92
Teaching, implication of brain
    research for, 143–156
Technology-enhanced learning,
    95–96
Test anxiety, 23–24
Thalamus, 34–35, 35
Tootell, Roger, 113

Triarchic mind model, 60
Tryptophan, 43

Unifying principles, 151–152
Unintended sameness, learning,
    146
Uvnas-Moberg, Kerstin, 52
Vasopressin, 53
Visual cortex, 132
Visual motor problems, 124
Visual perception, 124
Visual processing system, 106–107

Werner, Emmy, 48
Wernicke's area, 107, 114
Whole child, education of, 29
Whole language, 127
Whole learning, 6
Wiesel, Torsten, 15
Wingert, Pat, 119–128
Withdrawal behaviors, 36
Working memory, 23
Wynn, Karen, 134–135

Yale Summer Psychology
    Program, 73

Notes

Notes

Notes